William Croswell Doane, George Franklin Seymour

An Open Letter to the Rt. Rev. William C. Doane

In Reference to the Consecration of the Rt. Rev. Dr. Brooks

William Croswell Doane, George Franklin Seymour

An Open Letter to the Rt. Rev. William C. Doane
In Reference to the Consecration of the Rt. Rev. Dr. Brooks

ISBN/EAN: 9783337109714

Printed in Europe, USA, Canada, Australia, Japan

Cover: Foto ©ninafisch / pixelio.de

More available books at **www.hansebooks.com**

AN OPEN LETTER

TO THE

RT. REV. WILLIAM C. DOANE

(BISHOP OF ALBANY)

IN REFERENCE TO THE

CONSECRATION OF THE RT. REV. DR. BROOKS,

(BISHOP OF MASSACHUSETTS.)

BY THE

BISHOP OF SPRINGFIELD.

LETTER OF THE ARCHBISHOP TO CANON CARTER, RELATIVE TO THE CASE OF THE REV. VANCE SMITH.

"I confess that I do not understand the frame of mind that would lead a teacher of religion to protest against the Nicene Creed, and at the same time to join in a solemn service of which that Creed and its doctrines form, from the beginning to the end, so prominent a part. Neither can I understand any one feeling it right to invite to our Communion Service a teacher of the Unitarian body which so protests."

—LIFE OF ARCHBISHOP TAIT, Vol. 2, p. 70.

SPRINGFIELD, ILL.:
THE H. W. ROKKER PRINTING HOUSE.
1892.

COPYRIGHTED 1892, BY GEORGE F. SEYMOUR.

CONTENTS.

	PAGES
PREFATORY NOTE-	
Reasons for delaying the publication of the letter—Why it is not worth while to present the Bishop of Massachusetts for trial—The real issue at stake....................	1–3
THE OPEN LETTER TO BISHOP DOANE.............................	5–43
1. Reasons for addressing Bishop Doane......................	5
2. Reasons for publishing the open letter......................	6, 7
3. The Rev. Dr. Brooks' theological position made manifest by himself for years.....................................	8–10
4. The Rev. Dr. Brooks' course as a clergyman of the Church irreconcilable with his belief in the doctrine of the Trinity..	10, 11
5. The Church clear and decisive in her formularies on this and other points....................................	11, 12
6. The steps which the Bishop of Springfield took to secure the Church as to the soundness of faith of the Bishop-elect before consecration.................................	13, 14
7. Embarrassment occasioned by the secrecy maintained by the Bishops, who have charge of the voting, after the result was reached—the system faulty—remedies proposed........	14, 15
8. The cases of the Bishops of Hereford and Exeter in England—Bishop Doane's extraordinary method of reasoning.........	15–17
9. Bishop Doane's constituency immense; Why?..............	16
10. Demas and St. Luke types of character.....................	18–20
11. Our times test men, and compel them to show their real character	19
12. The philosophy of the day careless of truth—Calvinism responsible for a great deal of this laxity in the realm of truth..	21

OPEN LETTER—*Continued.*

PAGE.

13. Illustration of this tendency in the "charitable hypothesis" theory, touching regeneration in the Baptismal Office 22–25

14. The effect of this immoral treatment of the declarations of the Church of God leads to the Cummins Schism 23

15. Further effects in the free handling of God's word; the fluxing the Creed and Offices with new meanings, and the denial of the verities of the Gospel............................ 26

16. The interpretation theory as applied by certain men in theology, if put in practice by them in business would probably consign them to prison................................ 27

17. "Closed Questions." Christ and His Apostles and the Catholic Church have closed them........................... 27–29

18. The episcopate past and present one. Its testimony settles forever for churchmen the fundamental truths of revelation. 29

19. Partisanship to be distinguished from fidelity to the central truth of Christianity. The issue in the Bishop Brooks controversy is whether Christ in His Person is eternal or a creature. The charge of partisanship is unfounded in fact. 30, 31

20. The principles on which men administer trusts in business affairs reversed by some Bishops in dealing with the case of Bishop Brooks.......................... .... 31, 33

21. The precedent which the case of the Bishop of Massachusetts establishes for the future................................ 33, 34

22. The argument urged by certain Bishops from precedent in favor of confirming Bishop Brooks, thrown into a syllogism. The fallacy of such reasoning..................... 34–36

23. The Bishops who gave consent to Bishop Brooks' consecration, condemn their own action in their declaration on Christian Unity, and, in some instances, in individual utterances...................................... .... 37, 38

24. The constituency and commendations of Bishop-elect Brooks must distress all conservative Christians................. 38

25. The position of the Bishop of Springfield touching this Consecration restated...................................... 39, 40

26. Frightful illustrations of anomia and disloyalty exhibited by Clergymen in the Church 41

OPEN LETTER—*Continued.*   PAGE.

27. The real root issue involved in this Consecration, unless retraction is made or satisfactory explanation is given, is Christ or antichrist 42,43

APPENDICES.

APPENDIX I. The Bishop of Springfield's Circular Letter, addressed to all the Bishops exercising jurisdiction in the United States, as a warning to investigate the teaching and practice of the Rev. Dr. Brooks, before giving consent to his Consecration,.... 45-47

APPENDIX II. Letters addressed by the Bishop of Springfield to the Rev. Dr. Brooks, with a view to obtain from the Bishop-elect such explanations as would clear up the case.—The Rev. Dr. Brooks' replies 48-56

APPENDIX III. Letter addressed to the Presiding Bishop, urging him to approach the Rev. Dr. Brooks to obtain some retraction or explanation 57-59

APPENDIX IV. Protest of the Bishop of Springfield against the Consecration of the Rev. Dr. Brooks............................. 60,61

APPENDIX V. Unitarian Baptism of the Rev. Dr. Brooks.—Damaging commendations.. 62-67

APPENDIX VI. Pelagianism.—The Rev. Dr. Brooks' avowal of his holding this teaching.—This teaching in conflict with Holy Scripture and the Church.—The Rev. F. W. Robertson's erroneous teaching.—Answer to the same.—Excuse made for the Bishop of Massachusetts would not be accepted in any other sphere of life. 68-77

APPENDIX VII. Arianism.—Letters of the Rev. Dr. E. E. Hale and the Rev. Dr. James Freeman Clarke.—Remarks on the same.—Archbishop Tait's testimony, and that of the Convocation of Canterbury 78-90

APPENDIX VIII. Apostolical Succession.—Bishop Brooks' avowed position in regard thereto.—Quotations from Prayer Book and Canons.—The gift of life on every hand comes to us from the Life Giver by succession.................................... 91-97

PAGE.

APPENDIX IX. "Closed Questions": A Pastoral Letter of the Bishop of Springfield to his Diocese, showing that for Churchmen there are, by their own consent, questions that are forever settled..... 98–108

APPENDIX X. Declaration of the Bishops of the American Church on Christian Unity, at the General Convention of 1886............109–111

APPENDIX XI. Illustrations of Bishop Brooks' course in word and deed since his Consecration..112–121

APPENDIX XII. Bishop Doane on the "alleged invitation," as he calls it, given to Unitarian Ministers by the Rev. Dr. Brooks, and on Religious Orders, and the Rev. F. W. Puller's reply in London Guardian, with remarks.......................................122–133

APPENDIX XIII. Partisanship alleged by certain Bishops as a charge against those who opposed the Consecration of Bishop Brooks. The charge refuted..134–141

APPENDIX XIV. The apparent haste with which the arrangements for the Consecration of the Rt. Rev. Dr. Brooks were made and announced.—A remarkable paragraph from the New York Times, with Bishop Doane's explanation....................................142–144

CONCLUSION AND NOTE..144–148

PREFATORY NOTE.

This letter would have been printed long ere this had I not waited to see whether the suggestion of his friends, when they were urging the confirmation of the Bishop-elect of Massachusetts, on the ground that when he became a Bishop he would improve and show himself a different man, would be verified in the event.

I have waited in vain. This assurance of his friends, so monstrous in itself, that one who has proved disloyal in subordinate positions would become faithful and true when advanced to a higher office and entrusted with greater responsibilities, generated a hope, which has proved utterly fallacious. The Bishop of Massachusetts has not improved, and the Boston press has in effect told us "we knew as much all along, when his friends were urging Dr. Brooks' confirmation under the assurance that he would make a change in his teaching and conduct when he was consecrated a bishop. Dr. Brooks is not the man to alter his convictions or his conduct. We knew as much all along." Such is the sneer with which the friends of Bishop Brooks comment upon his acts and words of anomia now that he is the Bishop of Massachusetts.

I have not been deceived. I knew full well what was coming. But it was wise to wait, since it might have been claimed by the same deluded friends of the Bishop of Massachusetts, who were loud and persistent in saying, "make him a Bishop and he will cease to utter and do what shocked the Church when he was a Presbyter," it might have been claimed by them and others, that I had printed my letter before he had time or opportunity to show his character as a Bishop in the Church of God.

Ten or eleven months have elapsed since Dr. Brooks was consecrated, and by word and deed he has endorsed all that he said and did as a Presbyter.

Again it may be said, why not present the Bishop of Massachusetts for trial? I answer, because in his case it seems to me utterly useless, since on the authority of a Bishop, who has better opportunities for knowing whereof he affirms than most of his brethren enjoy, two-thirds of the Bishops of the Protestant Episcopal Church in the United States gave consent to Dr. Brooks' consecration. They knew full well Dr. Brooks' position as a fautor of Unitarians, as an avowed Pelagian, and one who repudiated with something of scorn and pity for those who held it, the doctrine of the Sacred Ministry as embodied in our Ordinal. They knew all this, and yet the Presiding Bishop, and with him a majority of the Bishops say, as in the presence of God, and awaiting the just judgment of God, "let him be made a Bishop, we do not consider these acts unrepented of, these words unretracted or unexplained inconsistent with his making the promises of the Ordinal and taking the Episcopal oath."

Is there any hope that these Bishops, possibly two-thirds of the American Episcopate, who say in 1891, let him be made a Bishop, will in 1892 consent to his condemnation? It would be stultification pure and simple.

God knows what awaits our Church. The outlook is distressing, numbers may increase, money may accumulate, temporal prosperity may abound, but the faith is dying out, truth, honor, manhood are at a discount. Cerinthus is in the splendid bath-house with its soft appointments of luxury and voluptuousness and ease, but St. John has fled poor, homeless, naked, Patmos awaits him, and the boiling oil, and a long, long life of confessorship. May God give me grace to endure whatever He may allow to be visited upon me for doing in my poor and humble way all that I can to maintain the faith once delivered to the Saints, and to uphold the order and discipline of the Church of Christ.

My contention in the pages which follow is not that Bishop Brooks is wrong in his Arianism, Pelagianism, and Congregationalism, but that, as holding these convictions, he has no right to remain in the Ministry of the Church, which condemns in its authoritative declarations such teaching. He has no right, moral right, to enter the Ministry, advance to its highest place and remain in it with a view to upset its foundations, reverse its ecumenical decisions, and turn it literally upside down. He has no moral right to do this, since meanwhile, until he accomplishes his purpose, he is obliged to say that he believes what he does not believe, and take part in offices and functions which he regards as worse than childish folly. I cannot reconcile such a position with moral rectitude and manly honor.

G. F. S.

SPRINGFIELD, ILL., Sept. 1. 1892.

AN OPEN LETTER

To the Bishop of Albany in Reference to the Consecration of the Bishop of Massachusetts,

THE RT. REV. DR. BROOKS.

Rt. Rev. and Dear Brother:

You need feel no surprise at my selection of yourself, as the public recipient of this letter, however much you may be unprepared for its appearance at this time, and from my hand. As a friend I can address you without the suspicion of personal ill feeling; as one with whom in large degree I have been in the past in theological accord, I am free from the imputation of partisan bias, and as making yourself, though late on the field, conspicuously active and zealous in promoting the confirmation and consecration of the present Bishop of Massachusetts, you commend yourself to me as the one of our Brethren, whom I ought without any hesitation to associate with myself before the public in the statement, which follows.

I am fully aware, my dear Brother, of the grave responsibility, which I assume in taking this step, but I am as fully convinced of the obligations, which impel me, as a Bishop in the Church of God, to take it.

I have done my utmost to avert the sad necessity, which now shuts me up to this last resource, as circumstances have shaped themselves and events have occurred, to free my conscience, and vindicate my honor.

The imputation has been repeatedly made, and more frequently implied, that those, who were opposed to the consecration of the Bishop of Massachusetts, on the basis, on which he was known to stand as a Presbyter, without retraction or explanation, had not the courage of their convictions, and were afraid to speak out, and this suggestion I have felt more keenly, since our dear Brother of Western Michigan seemed to stand alone before the public in wielding his pen and lifting his voice against the consecration as it took place, and it seemed pusillanimous that others, who shared his convictions and sympathies should keep silence. But even these considerations would not have determined me to address the Church at large, were it not, that as the case now stands, the safeguards, which surround the Episcopate in our land, have received, as a considerable number of the Bishops believe, a blow, which weakens them, and prepares the way for stifling, if not silencing the witness, which we must bear, if we are true to our Master, to the faith once delivered unto the saints. You yourself epitomise the danger, when you say in your address to your convention of 1891, "For myself I am free to say, that knowing a man to be honorable and responsible I should hesitate to refuse my consent to his consecration, if he were willing to take upon himself the solemn consecration vows." (Convention Address, p. 18.) On these terms with the views, which are accepted and advocated by a school, unhappily largely represented in our Church, you would admit to the Episcopate men, whose lips would take oaths, to which their hearts consented not, who would fill the old bottles with new wine, who would flux the creeds and offices with strange meanings, and avow, as they rose from their knees, interpretations, which would shock you. These men are reputed to be "honorable and responsible," and they avow and justify their course of action without reserve.

In view of such a chivalrous declaration as to your course in the future in admitting men to the Episcopate on the one hand, and the rapid increase of a school on the other, whose philosophy enables them without dishonor, as they think, to set themselves free from the binding force of human speech as the expression of thought, you see how extremely important the force of a precedent becomes, and hence I am driven to the conclusion, that nothing short of the discussion upon which I now propose to enter, and the facts which I now proceed to submit in reference to this consecration, will free my mind from guilt in the realm of conscience and as awaiting the judgment of the last great day.

Under these impelling causes I am forced to speak out, and I feel, my dear Brother, that I am indebted to you in your frank and magnanimous avowal of your purpose, as touching your consent to future consecrations for the reason, which leads me to address this letter through your doubly honored name* to the whole Anglican Communion.

---

* The Rt. Rev. Dr. George Washington Doane, Bp. of New Jersey was the father of the Bishop of Albany.

I have said that I did my utmost to prevent the sad
necessity, which now constrains me to write this letter. I
will briefly recapitulate the course which I pursued and the
steps which I took in order to secure the Church against
the intrusion into our episcopate so far as I knew then,
and now know, of one, who repudiated her polity, contemned her faith, and showed little or no respect for
her law and order. My apprehensions, you will particularly observe, were grounded upon the Bishop-elect's OWN
ACTS AND WORDS, not upon hearsay evidence, or popular
rumor. I recognized the salient fact that for years the
distinguished Presbyter of Massachusetts had attracted to
himself the attention, and secured the sympathy of an immense constituency of people hostile to the polity of the
Church, and in large proportion repudiating what we consider *the fundamental verities of the Christian Faith*, by
proclaiming himself in word and deed as more liberal than
the system into which he had voluntarily entered, and under which he was allowed to live and serve in consequence
of the vows which he had deliberately taken, as he was admitted to Holy Orders, those namely of the diaconate and
of the priesthood. These acts and words were not few, but
many, they were not confined to one occasion, and a single
year, but they were conspicuously before the public for
many years, so that the name of the Bishop of Massachusetts was a tower of strength for the sectarian and the unbeliever in his assaults upon the Church, as represented in
her ordinal, and creeds, and offices, and articles, hence
while I was as ready as any one could be to acknowledge
all that was claimed by his ardent and enthusiastic ad-

mirers for the eminent Presbyter in question, I felt, and I was compelled to feel grave distrust as to his fitness to be admitted to the Episcopate. I am not saying that the Rt. Rev. Dr. Brooks was not in the abstract right in all that he has said and done, that is, I am not arguing the question whether Congregationalism, Arianism and Pelagianism be true or false, of course the Church Catholic condemns these teachings as errors, but I am saying that from the standpoint of the ordinal, creeds, offices and articles of the Church in their plain and obvious meaning, he was manifestly in a mistaken position, and hence distrust of his fitness for the Episcopate was forced upon me by his own course as a Presbyter of the Church, through many years of a very conspicuous ministry.

This case then, you will observe, was fundamentally distinct from any which has ever occurred in the history of our Church. There have been instances where opposition has been made on the ground of partisan antipathies and suspicions engendered by those prejudices, but the present is separated from all such by the fact that the candidate himself is the cause of all the painful doubt and misgiving, and the points involved are not, in any sense, questions which divide the Church into schools of thought, but issues which reach down to the bottom truths of Christianity.

If the Bishop-elect's religious convictions were to be interpreted by his words and deeds and associations running through a long series of years, then his theological position as to the incarnation seemed to be that of an *Arian* of some sort, as regards man's natural condition, that of a *Pelagian*, and as touching ecclesiastical polity, that of a *Congregationalist*.

It is inconceivable that any man of integrity and honor who really believed in the divinity of Jesus Christ, as expressed by the homoousion of the creed of Christendom, could allow one who denied that fundamental verity of fundamental verities to receive the Holy Communion at his hands. This is what the Rector of Trinity Church, Boston, as it is alleged, *habitually did*. I am not speaking of administering the Blessed Sacrament to one, who unexpectedly to the celebrant, presents himself at the Lord's Table. In that case, charity might suggest that the would be recipient had abandoned his heresy and came as a believer, however unlikely the supposition might be, but I am speaking of cases where the parties invited were known to be Unitarians, and were asked *as such* to come to the Holy Communion. Consider what this act involves, naught less than the grossest insult to the majesty of the Eternal Son of God. Lower your thoughts infinitely from God to man and take an illustration from human experience of what such conduct means and see how you are shocked. Suppose the guardians of an earthly king or queen were to admit to the royal drawing room some one who they knew repudiated the character of the sovereign, and regarded the highest official personage in the state as a serf, and acted accordingly in the presence of majesty. How distressing such an exhibition would be. In the celebration of the Holy Eucharist, on any view of the Sacrament which you may take, allowable in the range of Catholic thought, you are in the presence chamber of the King of Kings, and He scrutinizes, not alone the outward man in dress and demeanor, but the secrets of the heart, and there by special invitation of the guardians of His honor are persons present, and who approach His throne, who deny His incommunicable glory and assert that He is a creature. They sink Him from the uncreated essence of deity by an infinite degradation to the level of created life. This is inconceivably worse than to allow the Queen of Great Britain to be treated as a char-woman, or the President of the United States as a day-laborer. What I am saying does not reflect upon the Unitarians, or the Arians, since they certainly may feel themselves justified in accepting an invitation when it is extended to them. The fault lies at the door of the host, not with those who come at his bidding as guests. Nor yet am I reflecting upon the host in this instance, except in so far as to suggest that in some unaccountable way he has been all along and is still, so far as I know, an Arian of some kind. On this theory, and it seems to me on no other, can his conduct be explained.

The Church has from the first guarded the Blessed Eucharist as practically the citadel of the Christian faith, and admission to Its reception ever has been and is regarded as the certificate, which may be seen and read of all men, of *orthodoxy*. The Anglican Communion is not behind the Church Catholic in the past, and of the present elsewhere in seeking to protect the Holy Mysteries from the intrusion of persons, who do not acknowledge the faith summed up in the creeds. The whole structure of the Liturgy, the rubrics, and the canons, and above all the recitation of the creed after the Gospel place a bar, which it would seem no honorable or responsible man who denied this faith would or could pass and present himself to receive at the Lord's Table. When I find therefore that a Presbyter, who has conspicuously on a great occasion invited persons whose public recognition is that of Unitarian ministers, to receive the Holy Communion in violation of the laws of the Church, and the essential spirit of the Liturgy, when I find that this Presbyter is a Bishop-elect, and is in prospect of being invested with the Episcopal office, and has made no retraction or explanation of such conduct and of numerous other acts and utterances of a like character, setting at defiance the authority of the Church as expressed in her ordinal, creeds, offices, articles, rubrics, and canons, then it becomes me, as one having the fear of God before his eyes, to endeavor as far as in me lies, to guard the trust of which I was put in charge, when I was made a Bishop, and to seek to set at rest all doubts and misgivings touching this Presbyter's orthodoxy, and loyalty to the polity and teaching of the Church, before he is consecrated.

This I strove to do in such ways as seemed to me available for the purpose, and I ceased not in my efforts until the act of consecration was performed. What has intensified my grief and distress has been that my Rt. Rev. Brethren, who gave their consent, seemed to be in possession of most, if not all of the facts, as they were known to me, and yet they said, "it pleases us that he should be a Bishop," nay some of them like yourself seemed to be eager that the Bishop-elect should be confirmed and consecrated, without one word of explanation, or apology.

I am aware of the delicacy which forbids a man to speak, while his case is still undecided, but when such restraint is removed by confirmation, then it would seem that he ought, if he could in conscience do so, to relieve the painful doubts and anxieties, which he himself has occasioned to thousands of his own household of faith.

I sought to bring this about by appealing to the Presiding Bishop as the one, who could with the most propriety approach the Bishop-elect and confirmed, and afford him an opportunity of explaining his past record, or of giving promise of amendment for the future. So far as I know, the Presiding Bishop did not see his way clear to do this, at all events the Bishop-elect was not heard from.

It is easy for you and others to criticise my acts in this sad business, but I submit that they were all honorable, and such as any one who believed in the essential divinity of his Saviour would take when he had good reason to be convinced that a man, who symbolized with Arius, was to be admitted to the Episcopate. The steps which I took were these:

1st. On the 16th of May I addressed a circular letter to my brother Bishops, urging them to consider what consent would imply unless some explanation were given. (See Appendix 1.)

2d. I addressed the Bishop-elect two letters explaining to him my position and difficulties, and asking him to relieve my anxieties. (See Appendix 2.)

3d. I addressed the Presiding Bishop after confirmation was secured, and received no reply. (See Appendix 3.)

4th. I sought to unite those, who refused consent, in a protest, to guard as far as possible the integrity of the Church, when she was receiving such a cruel blow, as it seemed to me, from her chief rulers—(Appendix 4)—and

5th. I send forth this letter in the hope that it will help to stay the downward trend of faith and practice, and as far as possible prevent this consecration being drawn into a precedent, so that we shall not presently have every possible heresy represented in our Episcopate.

I ought to say here that I have been embarrassed in my efforts to discharge what seemed to me to be my duty to the Church, by the secrecy, which surrounds the voting of the Bishops. I could not learn who the non-placets were. The information was refused when I sought it that I might consult with them. I do not mean to imply that the withholding such information was personal to myself, it was doubtless in accordance with the present system, but the present system is vicious in many of its details, and it ought to be recast and reformed throughout. Leaving out of view the relation of standing committees to Episcopal elections, which according to the most recent interpretation amounts to a mere shadow, and carries with it little or no weight or value, the responsibility of confirming Bishops-elect rests where it belongs with the Bishops of the Province, that is in our case with the Bishops exercising jurisdiction in the United States. We ought then to be put in a position by provision of law, where we could intelligently and rightly meet our obligations, and discharge our duty. We are not, however: on the contrary our condition is pitiable. We are left alone, each to act for himself as best he may, and if there be, as the occasion which draws forth this letter shows there may be, cases which cause grave doubts as to the fitness of the Bishop-elect for consecration, we are shut out from all means of allaying our anxieties and removing our scruples, and onward until consecration there is no opportunity afforded for applying any test, to secure the Church against the intrusion of men into the highest office of her ministry, who may seem to be scarcely apt and meet for such exalted station. If under such circumstances individual Bishops act or speak under the stress of conscience, they are liable to be misunderstood, at all events a hostile public press will put upon their conduct the worst possible construction and hold them up to ridicule and abuse. Again, the mode of signifying assent or dissent is open to criticism. A limit as to time should be set as to the period within which votes must be given, and every one should be by canonical obligation obliged to make response in the affirmative or negative, or saying unprepared to vote. Then until all the suffrages have been received the utmost secrecy should be observed, and when the result is reached, then the secrecy should be removed, and whoever wishes should be allowed to know how the vote stood and who the ayes and nays and neutrals were.

The attempt has been made to soften the present case upon which I am commenting, by bringing under review two instances which have occurred within the present century in our Mother Church of England—those, namely, of the Bishop of Hereford, in 1848, and of the Bishop of Exeter, in 1869—which occasioned, at the time when they respectively occurred, grave apprehensions, on account of the alleged heterodox teaching of the parties nominated by the Crown to those sees.

In the first place, I desire to draw your attention to the unusual direction which your inference takes when arguing about the things of God, and respectfully inquire whether it would take the same direction if you were considering your own affairs? The argument seems to be this: Persons, whose past career has awakened grave misgivings, have been admitted to the Episcopate, and no alleged positive ill results have followed in their case; consequently we may infer that no evil will be produced in the future by continuing to allow such consecrations. Suppose there were forced into your schools two pupils of depraved habits, and it so happened that the scholars, so far as you knew, were not harmed, would you recognize that as a reason for continuing to run the risk of admitting immoral pupils in the future? If you did, I fear your patrons would not agree with you, and your schools would soon be empty.

In the second place, the Church of England is not responsible, as you know full well, for the choice and consecration of her Bishops, as we are in this country. The State, it may be said, controls the whole business. The Crown nominates, and forces its nominee upon the Church, under the threat, if the Church declines to receive the person named, of the pains and penalties of praemunire, which amount to outlawry. When Bishop Hampden was consecrated, the State showed her teeth, and Dean Meriweather and even Bishops quailed. Lord John Russell showed little courtesy or consideration to the highest dignitaries of the

Church in that day. The Church in these United States labors under no such apprehensions, and consequently she is free to act, and her responsibility to God and man is correspondingly the greater.

Again, the cases of the Bishops of Hereford and Exeter must be separated, since they are really wide apart. Dr. Hampden was censured for pravity of teaching, but it was urged in his defense that he was by nature incapable of recognizing theological distinctions; that, as in the field of vision there are persons who are color-blind, so, in the sphere of theology, the unfortunate Regius Professor of Divinity was color-blind; he could not tell green from red. He was in heresy, but he did not know it.

Dr. Temple, once Bishop of Exeter, now Bishop of London, was never censured in person. The utmost that can be said of him was, that he was in questionable company. The book of Essays in which his appeared, was condemned. Had his essay been separated from its companions, no fault could or would have been found with it. Leaving out of view differences of country and state control, the cases of Hereford and Exeter do not approach a parallel with the case of Massachusetts.

In writing as I do, I am well aware of my present disadvantage as compared with the position which you occupy. I must appeal simply to Churchmen—to those who accept the faith and polity of the Church, and are in hearty sympathy with the rubrics and canons which guard the Catholic Creed and Apostolic Order. Your strength lies beyond, in the great multitude, who applaud what they call liberality, and who imagine that truth has no real existence beyond a man's own thoughts. Your constituency is immense; mine is small. I am content. I pass to discuss other matters.

There are times which "try men's souls." Times which, so to speak, turn men inside out, and reveal to the world of what stuff they are made. Often the disclosure, when the excitement is over and the crisis is past, astonishes no one more than the very men who have exceeded, or disappointed expectations, as the case may be. Doubtless the wretched Demas, who had once stood manfully for the cause of Christ in the face of danger, was amazed at himself when, confronted by the prospect of the Neronic persecution, he forsook the aged Apostle in his Roman prison, having loved this present world more than truth, and honor, and duty. Probably the blessed evangelist, St. Luke, who had shared with Demas the holy companionship of St. Paul, was equally surprised when he found himself the subject of universal commendation for his patient continuance in well doing. One event had happened alike to both. The one quailed and fell; the other went right on as he had done before. The crisis tested them, and we, you and I and all men, *know them now as Demas and St. Luke.* Their names have not been changed, but the men who bear those names are now seen through them as *they really are*—the time-server and the coward on the one hand, and the steadfast friend and hero on the other.

Ordinarily men are not tried in this manner. They go on the even tenor of their way, and pass out of this world without being compelled to give an account of themselves to their own souls, or to others about them. That ordeal awaits them when, at the bar of final judgment, they must come forth from their hiding place, and each, in the Apostle's language, "give account of himself to God." Perhaps we ought to be thankful when the heavens gather blackness over our heads, and we find ourselves in the storm, or see that it will very soon burst upon us, because such experiences anticipate the judgment day, and show us ourselves as we really are. The disguise is stripped off, and in mercy we are compelled to see ourselves as God sees us.

Whether it be for our own advantage or not, such providentially is our lot to find ourselves, at the close of this century, in times which subtly test men, and bring their innermost self to the surface and display it. The test is not applied, as in the age of Demas and St. Luke, with pain and suffering and death. It comes now in another form, rather the opposite. The devil is not personified in Nero, but comes arrayed as an angel of light. He is a liar still, he must always be, but his lie is no longer black with the horrid immorality portrayed by St. Paul in his Epistle to the Romans, and exhibited as the staple of every-day life in that old heathen world. Satan has now insinuated himself into the very strongholds of Christianity, and sought to enter into a truce with its leaders and militant hosts. He reaches or rather overreaches multitudes of excellent and deeply religious people through a vain philosophy, which allies itself with the Gospel, and seduces men into accepting its sophistry, by professing the profoundest love for the Saviour, while it robs Him of His glory; the deepest reverence for the dogmatic faith, while it divests it of its truth; and the greatest respect for its official ministry, while it denies the grace of orders.

Its method is not altogether new; it was employed with success in Athens, in the days of Socrates. He unsparingly exposed it, and scourged it in his encounters with the Sophists. It has always been in the world since it played fast and loose with words in the Garden of Eden, and whispered, as it impiously and blasphemously gave God the lie, "Ye shall not surely die." It always has been in the world, and doubtless always will be, but now it strengthens itself in a condition of things which has never existed before, and takes advantage of weapons forged for a very different purpose, which are ready for use and near at hand.

The conditions of life are so improved that the world has improved with age, and men like it better than they did. Mammon is a mightier god than ever he was before. His worship invites conclusions, which men are only too ready and eager to adopt—such as the unreality of sin, the uselessness of sacrifice, the aimless love of God, saving all irrespective of spiritual condition, without penitence and without faith.

It would have been difficult for this Epicurean philosophy to intrude itself into any system, which professedly rested upon the Gospel of Jesus Christ, much less into the bosom of the Catholic Church, had a way not been prepared for its admission, and weapons contrived for its defence centuries ago, when Calvinism found lodgment in the minds and hearts of multitudes in the West, and imposed its blighting influence upon the Church itself and the Word of God. The formulated principles of Calvinism, as laid down with consummate ability by its author, are absolutely and manifestly irreconcilable with Holy Scripture, and the dogmatic teaching of historic Christianity. To overcome this apparently insuperable obstacle to the entrance, and more, the acceptance of "the five points," as they were called, of this system in the region of thought and belief, which claimed Christ as their author, a contrivance was resorted to, which served for the time very satisfactorily, but which, like all dishonest and immoral methods has wrought and is working incalculable mischief. It was not, of course, the intention of those who had recourse to this clever device to do harm. They thought that they were doing God service in making it possible for the cherished teaching of their master to be reconciled, as they fondly persuaded themselves it was, by what they called "interpretation," to the Gospel of Jesus Christ.

With this machinery, for with the elder Calvinists "interpretation" covered a great deal of ground, they achieved success. Interpretation included exegesis, exposition, application, parallelism, correllation of texts, and sometimes, when naught else would do, the absolute rejection of the written word, calling it as did Luther the Epistle of St. James, "a scripture of straw." This ingenious machinery enabled these magicians to accomplish wonders with the Bible, the Creed and the Church. The language remained the same, but it was fluxed with new meanings, draped with new expositions, explained away with brand new hypotheses, which they called without appreciating in the remotest degree the irony of the expression, "*charitable*." A single illustration will serve to make plain my meaning.

and I choose it the rather, because it shows how much mischief is caused by tampering with truth. One of the chief tenets of Calvinism is *the indefectibility of grace*, that is that grace once received cannot be forfeited, it must accomplish its purpose and bring its subject, the one who has received it, to salvation in heaven. The baptismal office of the Church asserts of every one baptized that "he is regenerate," or born again, but the theory of John Calvin compels this language to mean, that every such person pronounced regenerate is absolutely and unconditionally sure of ultimate salvation. We know, however, by sad experience that many who are baptized lead bad lives and die impenitent, and consequently it is abhorrent to reason, and the moral sense to teach that such reprobates will be saved. What then? Must Jesus Christ and his Church give way, or John Calvin? They are manifestly brought into direct conflict, since our Blessed Lord clearly teaches that baptism and the gift of regeneration are united, and the Church applies His teaching in her office. "Except a man be born of water and of the Spirit he cannot enter into the Kingdom of God," are Christ's express words, and another injunction of His is, "What God hath joined together let not man put asunder." Accordingly Christ's body, the Church, speaking in His Name, says of every one who is baptized, "Seeing now dearly beloved brethren that this person is regenerate." And John Calvin rejoins, "it is not certain, far from it; it is very doubtful." How then is such a colossal difficulty to be surmounted? By the theory of a "*charitable hypothesis*," which is another name for "*interpretation*," by fluxing the words of the baptismal office. which are positive, and assert without qualification a thing as being so, as being true, by fluxing them with a new meaning, so that they are to be understood in a new sense. The Church says, "is regenerate," but the Church does not know how to express herself. She means, says Calvinism, that "the person may charitably be supposed to be regenerate, but it is by no means certain." That is to say, Holy Church, our Mother, meets us at the font with a lie, or a quasi lie. She assures us of what she is not sure. She tells us positively and without any qualification that a thing is true, which she does not know to be true—nay, which, if she is as wise as was John Calvin, she has grave reasons for believing is more likely to be false than true. This is a specimen of what is called "interpretation" as employed in times before our day, and inherited by us with all its baleful effects of disloyalty to truth, laxity of belief, evasion and conjuring with words. No wonder a schism resulted as a protest against being obliged, by ordination vows, to utter in the name of God, as truth, what at best was not, as they were taught and believed, certainly true. One feels a pity for such persons, and, to a certain extent, a sympathy for them, since if we were laboring under the misapprehension which seemed to be their fatality, we certainly could not have repeated those words as they stand in the office. At all events, these persons ought to be given credit for honesty and honor. When they found themselves unable to accept what they, under misconception, supposed to be the teaching of the Church, they left the Church. They did not remain and strive, by evasion and trickery and disloyalty, to reform the Church, or flux the Church with their individualisms as new meanings, which would lift the Church to the level, as they express it, of the age, by which they mean, in their unbounded self-conceit, *their own level.*

The misconception of these misguided men arose from the new meaning or interpretation which Calvinism had put into the word "regeneration." In the Catholic sense, it means the second or new birth,—*it is an event, a fact,* as was the first birth. It introduces its subject into a new condition or state, with possibilities unnumbered and unlimited. It runs a parallel, therefore, with our natural birth, as our Lord clearly teaches, by using the language which He employs. Natural birth is a fact, an event: the child is born once for all. It may be a misshapen monster, it may come into the world with inherited disease, it may die as soon as it is born, or it may live and be a curse upon the earth—nevertheless it is born, and the midwife is entitled to say, "this child is born, and it comes into this world as the gift of God," just as truly as when it is perfect in limb and form, and developes into a saint. After the same manner the second or spiritual birth *is a fact, an event;* it occurs once for all. The divine instrument of this birth is the Holy Ghost, but the Holy Ghost is not the gift of baptism. He, the Blessed Spirit, is the gift of the laying on of hands in Confirmation. Whether the subject of the second birth comes qualified or not, when he is baptized the Church, like the midwife, proclaims a fact, and says, "this person is regenerate." No worse case could occur, it is difficult to believe, than that of Simon Magus, who meets us on the threshold of Christianity, and yet after his baptism, although St. Peter tells him that he is still "in the gall of bitterness and the bond of iniquity," he does not bid him be baptized again, any more than he counsels him to enter a second time into his mother's womb and be born, but he exhorts him *to repent*. Had Simon repented at the preaching of St. Peter, and not gone on still in his wickedness, he would have made the possibilities of the spiritual life his glorious possession and have been saved. If then it was true of Simon Magus, when he was baptized that he was regenerate, it is equally true of every one. But Calvin fluxed regeneration with the logical consequences of his own original system, and hence he overflowed the word with renovation, sanctification and salvation, and of course with such an interpretation it would not be certainly true that the subject of Baptism was regenerate, any more than it would be true to assert, that because a child was born into this world it would be a great and good man.

But the misery of this immoral treatment of Holy Scripture, and the teaching of Holy Church, of making the Word of God of none effect by human inventions and interpretations, which is a trifle worse than by traditions, the misery is that it has borne its bitter and pernicious fruit, and taught succeeding generations to go forward on the lines of their ancestors, and as they would say, improve upon their methods. Now we have men who lay claim to the highest positions in the Church, who unblushingly contemn her orders, compromise her deposit of faith by word and deed, break with the fellowship of the Apostles, which was one of the criteria of the first believers, and rejoice in the

companionship of a great multitude, who have only one
thing in common, that they disown the Catholic heritage
as it comes to us from the past, held and administered by
a living Episcopate, and enshrined in creed and office and
ordinal. The one word these men use in their defense is,
"interpretation." It is the old word, the charitable hypothesis idea made to do new service in undermining the Word
of God, traversing the creed with strange and false meanings, breaking down the bulwarks of the Church in sacred
office, in rubrical and canonical law, reducing her, the vineyard of the Lord, to a wretched common. With their "interpretation," as they call it, they assail the fundamental
verities of the faith in a multitude of words, which, like
the haze which envelopes the mountains, half conceals their
destructive and deadly purpose. Under this process of
criticism the doctrine of the Blessed Trinity, the homoousion of the Eternal Son with the Father, His supernatural
birth of the Virgin Mary, the atonement made by the shedding of the precious Blood, the resurrection of the body,
the ministries of the Holy Ghost in the three sacred orders,
and in the sacraments and means of grace, all are evaporated
into refinements, which mean nothing, and Christianity is
reduced to a bare *humanitarianism*, a system to promote
good living here on earth and ameliorate the woes and ills
to which flesh is heir. Press such men with the venerable
truths, as they stand in the creed and liturgy of the ages,
and the proof texts of the old Bible, and they will lift their
eyebrows with supercilious scorn, and tell you the new interpretations of the scholars of to-day, the theologians

who get their inspiration from infidels and agnostics, scatter all such rubbish to the winds.

The wonder grows upon us how people of good sense and honesty of purpose can be imposed upon by such transparent sophistry. Take these men, who are playing fast and loose with truth in the domain of theology, into any other sphere of life, and let them there exhibit their ingenuity at their game of interpretation, and they will very speedily come to grief. Let them try the experiment, say in the matter of contracts or finance, and the patience of their fellow-men would soon be exhausted in dealing with such triflers, and they would justly stand, ere long, to plead to indictments laid against them for fraud—nay, they might be convicted and placed as felons behind prison bars.

I am quite well aware that there are cases, and very many, where there is room for varieties of interpretation, but I am also equally well aware that those cases never include, *for Churchmen*, "the closed questions" of revelation and the Apostles' and Nicene Creeds. (See Appendix 9.) Christ made no provision, in His charter of government, for amendment or repeal at the pleasure of mankind. His injunction to the Apostles is to teach on His authority whatsoever He had commanded them, and the limits and metes and bounds of *this imposed faith* were fixed by those to whom he gave the pledge and promise that the Holy Ghost would bring all things which He had told them to their remembrance, and would guide them into all truth. The fundamental principles of the polity, faith, sacraments and worship of the Church were settled forever by these inspired men before they were taken out of this world. Hence it could be said, and is said by the Word of God, that the first believers "continued steadfastly in the *Apostles*' doctrine, and fellowship, and in the breaking of bread, and in prayers." Essentially these things have never been changed from that day to this, and it is our great privilege and honor to hold them as a sacred trust for ourselves and all men, if they will share with us in the divine legacy, and to be permitted, if we show ourselves worthy, to transmit them *inviolate* to those who are to come after us. If the form of sound words which St. Paul bade St. Timothy "hold fast," has received any additions since his day, it has not been in the way of enlarging the body of revealed truth, that can only be done by Him, Who originally revealed the truth, but it has been with a view to define the truth, *already held in possession as a trust*, against new interpretations (that is the word), which were calculated to undermine and destroy the truth. The Creed is no larger now, as regards the area of truth which it covers, than it was when St. Paul quoted three of its articles in writing to the Church of Corinth: "I delivered unto you first of all," he says, "that which I also received, how that Christ died for our sins according to the Scriptures, and that He was buried, and that He rose again the third day according to the Scriptures." (1 Corinth. xv. 3, 4.) As St. Paul received it, so we have received it. It is no more ours than it was his; it is a precious, sacred deposit placed in our hands as a *trust*, and we are forbidden to tamper with it ourselves, or allow others to tamper with it.

It was one of the purposes of the Blessed Master in vesting the polity of His Church in a *corporation*, the apostolate, that it should guard His truth and carry it to the ends of the earth, and preserve it inviolate for all time. "Ye shall be witnesses unto Me," our Lord says to His Apostles, "both in Jerusalem and in all Judaea, and in Samaria and unto the uttermost part of the earth." He made them partners in *a joint trust*, and committed unto them heavenly treasures, precious beyond measure, the gift of orders, the offices which represent Him, the faith once for all delivered unto the saints, the sacraments, the official channels of His grace and divine worship, arranged in accordance with the analogy of faith. This sacred deposit is to be guarded and handed on and down from generation to generation and age to age, and security taken for its safe transmission. As the Church grew and spread, and Bishops were multiplied, the aggregate of witnesses who had gone up higher, added to those who remained on earth, became a majority so vast and so constantly increasing, that the voice of the collective Episcopate, departed and living, could not be overcome by the defection of one or two or ten or a hundred, who might drift into heresy and make shipwreck of their faith. They could not carry the Church, *as a whole*, with them into unbelief and schism, but they might compromise the Church in any one land and break with the mighty past and their brethren of the present. This unhappily has occurred and it may happen again. "Let him that thinketh he standeth take heed lest he fall." "He that hath an ear let him hear what the Spirit saith unto the Churches."

Recognizing the fact then that the Episcopate is put in charge of the Gospel (St. Paul calls the faith "the Gospel"), and recognizing the further fact that the faith is now assailed by a host of men, not only without the Church, but also within, who profess to hold the truth while they make it void by their interpretations, it becomes my duty to give account of myself to the Church, that I may not be thought remiss in those things which concern the whole body of the faithful, when the safety of the sacred deposit is threatened, and our claim as a branch of Christ's Church is weakened by an apparent condoning of disloyalty in conduct and error in teaching, which is profoundly distressing.

I am speaking of what passes beyond the limits of party lines. The distinction is almost too obvious to be dwelt upon at length, but inasmuch as confusion exists on this point in certain quarters, and the charge has been made of partisanship, it is worth while to remark that principles are one thing, and the application of those principles is quite another. Men may differ and do differ as to the best method of *administering* government, and in consequence separate into parties, and in the heat of controversy, in debate, and in legislation, and in the conduct of affairs exhibit, and may be justly charged with the offense of exhibiting partisanship, but when the *government itself* is assailed, when the *fundamental principles of the constitution are contemned and repudiated*, then resistence to such ruinous assaults is not partisanship, it is in the political world, *patriotism*, in the sphere of religion, *loyalty to truth and duty*. When a man fires upon the flag of my country, if I were a layman I would be prepared to fight ; when a man flatly contradicts the Blessed Lord Himself, and the teaching of the Prayer Book throughout its length and breadth, then as a Bishop in the Church of God I will resist as far as I can, and by every method which I can legitimately employ, strive to prevent the intrusion of such a person into a share of the custody of treasures, which he has held so cheap, that he counted them of no worth, and which, as worthless in his eyes, he wished to scatter to the winds, and if I fail in my efforts to protect the Church from such a disastrous compromise, of what seems to me to be her safety and honor, then, while I must perforce submit to the blow inflicted upon our communion, I will still do my best to break, as far as possible, its force. This is not partisanship, it has no relation to any party or school in the Church, it goes beyond all questions which separate men into high or low, or broad or narrow; it reaches down to the foundation, to the corner stone, *to Christ.*

Leaving then the charge of partisanship, which, like all personalities in a crisis like the present, sinks into insignificance, let us, my Brother, confront our duty as holding a trusteeship under Christ, of treasures of infinite worth, which He has placed in our hands, and ask ourselves the question, what principles ought to 'guide us in the administration of our stewardship?

We may safely say, and we think all right-minded people will agree with us, that we ought to be as jealous of our spiritual trusts as we would be of any mere earthly treasure committed to our custody, as, for example, money or children. It is not difficult to discover the way in which men view their duty in the care of their wealth or offspring. They see to it, as far as they can, when they are about to make a loan or contract a daughter in marriage, that the borrower or their prospective son-in-law is worthy. If there comes to their ears the faintest rumor that the one who is on the eve of taking their ten thousand dollars or fondly loved child is tarnished in reputation, to whom do they give the benefit of their doubt, to the petitioner for the gold or the wife, or to their money or the sunshine of their home? The question answers itself. The financier responds, "not one dollar goes out of my hands until I am satisfied that he who seeks it is above suspicion." The father replies, "I would sooner die than surrender my darling to one of whose honor I am not perfectly sure." The man who seeks a loan or a wife *is not claiming a right, he is asking a favor*, and hence it is for him to make good his cause by establishing his integrity. It is the unquestionable duty of the banker or the parent to look well to it that there is no ground for distrust, before they part with their treasures. To act upon any other principle, would be a criminal neglect or shirking of responsibility.

When we pass from human trusts to divine, from ordinary business men of the world to Bishops in the Church of God, what principles shall govern them in the administration of their stewardship? Shall they reverse the axioms of prudence, which guard the safety of earthly possessions and material interests, and give the benefit of the doubt, when grave suspicion is aroused and widely prevails, to the candidate pressed upon them for admission to their order, to share in the guardianship of their heavenly inheritance, and the responsibility of transmitting it unimpaired to their successors? Shall they say, in a careless, good-natured way, "it is true this man has been erratic in conduct and heretical in speech, but the Episcopal office will improve him; it has done so before; let us give him the benefit of the doubt and make him a Bishop"? One would antecedently suppose that it would be impossible that any man who was conscious that he was a trustee for God, and was living and acting under the restraint of an oath of fealty, could utter such sentiments, and carry them out in the act. Let us leave the matter there. It is better that we should.

The tremendous responsibility, my Brother, of our stewardship over and above the priceless value of the treasures which it guards, is increased, if it be possible, by the consideration that our conduct helps to make *a precedent* in the direction of laxity and demoralization and ruin. If the benefit of the doubt is given not to God's heritage, but to the man who knocks at the door and asks to share in the administration of that heritage which he has hitherto treated with habitual disrespect, then his consecration adds another illustration to strengthen the position of those who deal with God's trusts as they certainly never would with their own worldly affairs.

And still another kind of precedent is supplied by this reversal of the fundamental principles which govern men in caring for their own personal interests. Whatever defect in belief or idiosyncrasy of conduct may belong to a man who becomes a Bishop, it is claimed by those who are high in authority, that henceforth those negations of faith and eccentricities of behaviour cannot be urged in future as bars against admission to the Episcopate. In the face of such an allegation, how awful becomes the responsibility of consenting to the consecration of one, who not in a private way, but openly and defiantly and repeatedly, through long years of ministration, is reputed to have treated with little consideration the law of the universal Church, the rubrics of our Prayer Book, and the Ordinal, which protects while it confers the three-fold ministry, without one word of explanation or apology. Henceforth, then, no one can be refused who stands upon this level, and so the descent is easy, lower and lower.

The argument, of course, is fallacious. Thrown into a syllogism, it stands as follows, and its weakness at once appears.

Whatever a man admitted to the Episcopate believes, or does; or does not believe, or refuses to do, henceforth becomes a standard, and no one afterwards can be rejected who occupies the same position. This is the major premise. Now let us pass to the minor, and draw the conclusion. Certain Bishops, it is said, in England and in this country, have denied the necessity of Episcopal ordination or consecration as a qualification to minister the sacraments; consequently these Bishops have virtually *repealed the Ordinal*, for the weakest link measures the strength of the chain, and when all the Bishops on the bench hold the same view of the sacred ministry, and they may, then the Ordinal, with its preface, and the canons which guard it and give practical effect to it, would not remain one moment longer than it would be possible to repeal them and get rid of them. And, indeed, on the theory that Episcopacy is not of divine origin, and imposed by God upon the Church as His polity for its government, this would be what ought to be done, since in that view of the subject it is an intolerable impertinence to shut men out from our altars who have as valid a claim to represent Christ as we have. Could I be persuaded that the Ordinal does not mean what it says, that Episcopacy is not rooted in the charter of government given by Christ to His Apostles (St. Matt. XXVIII, 18. etc), and by them developed as He had prescribed, I would not, for I could not, remain in a system which, resting simply on human foundations, no matter how ancient they were, refused to recognize as ministers of Christ our brethren, who had as good a warrant for what they presumed to do as we could produce.

But to return to our syllogism and the consequences of recent action, which stare us in the face and confront our communion. It is not a matter of private opinion, which a man may hold and teach as his view, but it is an issue forced upon our attention by the public press representing not only religion, but secularity, sectarianism, and, worse, infidelity, so that the consent to admission, as the outside world distinctly claims, carries with it the necessity of acknowledging the faith once delivered unto the saints to be a matter indifferent, and the Ordinal, with its preface and its provisions for making Bishops, Priests and Deacons, to be useless, and indeed worse, an impertinence. The argument, then, of these excellent men brings us to these conclusions. Certain Bishops in the past, as holding lax views on the subject of Episcopacy, repealed the Ordinal, and now, much more, one who has made himself publicly conspicuous for discrediting the only purpose which the Ordinal can serve, and in addition has, by word and deed, discounted the fundamental verities of the blessed Gospel, has repealed the Apostles' and the Nicene Creeds.

Henceforth no man can be refused the Episcopate who treats the doctrine of the Blessed Trinity as a matter of no consequence, since, it can be urged, one has gone in with the consent of a majority of his Brethren, who knew, for the facts were distinctly brought to their attention, that by deed and word he had compromised the doctrine of the essential divinity of Jesus Christ. Thank God the reasoning is utterly fallacious and the conclusions fall to the ground. If such logic were to be allowed, it would follow that there was a place in our Episcopate for almost every heresy which has ever cursed the world, since there have been heretical Bishops of many kinds and names in the highest places in the Church. Nay, worse, we should be compelled to condone immorality, since Bishops, who must be nameless, have knelt to receive imposition of hands, who were thoroughly bad men. I am amazed, and more than amazed, that any man who holds the office of a Bishop could so far seem to forget his duty to God as a trustee, as to delude himself into the belief that he could throw the responsibility of his acts in the administration of his trust, and that too in its highest exercise, upon others, and say, "such and such men held these or similar views and were accepted, and hence I may give my approval without blame." Again, I say, no one would for one moment treat his own earthly trusts in this way. It is the reverse of worldly prudence in affairs, and I cannot conceive of any business being safely transacted on these terms. Nay,

Bishops themselves, when speaking theoretically, and not acting under the constraint of potent influences in specific cases, give forth no uncertain sound. Listen to the language of the report of the Bishops of our Church on Christian Unity, adopted unanimously in 1886. I add a portion of it as an appendix. (Appendix 10.) Listen again to such brave words as these which you yourself wrote, and with which the public are already familiar, since they met our eye daily during the months of *June and July*, of the last year at the bottom of the pages of our *Church Almanac*. Brave words they are, and they deserve to be perpetuated and sounded out so that all may hear them. "But, I believe," you say "that we are bound to remember two things. First, that *truth cannot be sacrificed to anything*. The danger in the Roman direction is to make light of truth, in dwelling much upon order, and the danger in the Protestant direction is to set schemes or species of union above truth," this for June; still better, if it be possible, for July. You tell us, and it braces one up to hear the noble words, "the fact is, that unless we maintain our *Order intact, and hold fast positively to every article of faith*, which the Church has set forth in the ancient Creeds, we have nothing whatever to offer those whom we seek to draw into closer oneness with ourselves. If these things are important, *they are trusts which we cannot surrender, no matter how tempting the proposal may be.*" These principles, so luminously stated in the Report on Christian Unity, and by yourself, who were speaking to thousands of Churchmen, by a singular coincidence, during the first two months of the summer of 1891, so valiantly for the maintenance of the Catholic faith and order at any cost, *these principles are true.*

It is a trite saying, that "a man is known by the company which he keeps." The fellowship of the *first believers was with the Apostles.*

It occasions some perplexity when a Churchman's constituency is made up chiefly of those who refuse the Catholic faith and reject the Apostolic Order, and whose commendation is sounded largely by alien voices, and in words not restrained by the reverence which animates those who were brought up in the school of liturgic worship. I am not speaking of social affiliations, but I have in mind theological sympathies, and I have been appalled with statements of laudation and approval from quarters and in language which must be, it would seem to me, exquisitely painful and distressing to one who found himself a Bishop in the Church of God.

Be it observed, my Brother, we are brought face to face with a fact which, antecedently, I could not have been persuaded to believe—that we have, with the consent of a majority of our Bishops, a presbyter admitted to the Episcopate without any apology, withdrawal or explanation, who has, by repeated utterances and acts, treated with little or no consideration the authority of the Church in her provisions for the guardianship of her faith and polity, and whose conduct and teaching in these respects have been matters of public notoriety for years, so that he has come, in consequence, to be regarded by the outside world as the great apostle of what it calls "Liberality."

At the risk of repeating myself, I desire to place on record my distinct and deliberate and unalterable position in reference to the issues involved in this consecration, until some retraction is made or satisfactory explanation is given. It is not in any sense, as I have said, a question of party. If it were, I should not have been found in the opposition with Bishops of every shade of theological opinion. If it were, I would justly discredit myself with others, and forfeit my own self-respect. Nor, again, is there one particle of personal feeling, which affects or qualifies my position. My relation to this matter would be the same were the party concerned my father or my brother. I am not conscious of aught but the kindest feelings towards him whose consecration I regard as most disastrous and injurious to our Communion. It is not his fault that he is where he is. *His acts and words have not been done or spoken "in a corner."* They have been the public property of the nation for years. And, once more, my refusal to consent and acquiesce is not based in the slightest degree upon what others have said or written; *it rests entirely upon the unquestioned deeds and statements of the eminent personage himself.* I do not say that his positions, as defined by what he has said and done, are in themselves wrong—that is a different question—but I am convinced that they are absolutely inconsistent with the Episcopal oath and vows, provided words, not here or there, but everywhere, are allowed to have their obvious and current meaning, and are not made of none effect by novel "interpretations."

I found myself, therefore, in the ordering of God's providence, compelled either to refuse consent to this consecration or to stultify myself—nay, worse, as I view the matter, I am speaking for myself, and mean no disrespect to others, and cannot be responsible for inferences. Nay, worse, I say, for we live, as Bishops, under the obligation of vows and a most solemn oath. I felt myself compelled either to refuse consent or to be disloyal to the trust committed to our keeping, and unfaithful to the Church of God, not simply in these United States, but to the Catholic Church throughout the world now militant upon earth, and more to the Church of the past—the Church of the Apostolic age, the Church of St. Cyprian, the Church of St. Chrysostom, and St. Gregory, and St. Augustine, the Church to which our Reformers appealed in their sharp trials of confessorship and martyrdom. I have not given pledges to the heterogeneous multitude made up of every conceivable sect and name, which has been shouting for months, "Consecrate him, consecrate him; if you do not consecrate him you are not the world's friend," but I have given pledges and an oath to the One Holy Catholic and Apostolic Church of the past, through the ages all along, and of the present, diffused throughout the earth, *to keep the faith undefiled, and maintain and hand on the threefold ministry.* I have never fluxed the Creed or the Ordinal with any theory or interpretation of my own. Who am I, that I dare be guilty of such monstrous presumption, of such an awful impiety?

The Creed and the Ordinal have stood in their essential principles the same from the beginning. The Catholic

Church has interpreted them, if they needed interpretation, by her practice in the ages all along. She has successfully resisted the private interpretations of Arius and Apollinarius, and Nestorius and Eutyches, and Honorius and Erigena, and Luther and Calvin, and she will resist these private interpretations to the end. But as in the past, so in the present, there is danger lest though the fickleness of the people or the pusillanimity and treason of her rulers, portions of the Lord's heritage should be surrendered to the enemy and lose their position as branches of the Catholic Church. This is our danger now. Men there are who stand forth as champions of negations, who refuse Moses and the Prophets, who discredit the Bible as the Word of God, who reject the Articles, who make the Creeds meaningless or worse by their interpretations, whose names insult Christianity as corresponding editors of infidel publications, and who inspire the godless multitude with an estimate of themselves, and the authority which is over them in the Lord, which is expressed in caricatures in comic newspapers, where surplice and stole and rochet and lawn sleeves are made the jest of thousands. These men wax bold and defiant when one of themselves, whose sympathy they enjoy passes into the Episcopate with the oath of conformity and the pledges of obedience of the Ordinal. There is danger, I say, imminent danger, of our Church losing her candlestick, and sinking in darkness out of communion with the Catholic Church into fellowship with those, who deny the Lord that bought them with His precious blood, and the blessed Trinity and the official ministry, and becoming, as she would be, and would earn for herself the degradation of being the most contemptible of sects. I have used every available means within my reach to avert this blow from our branch of the Church, and now that it has fallen, perhaps it may be my privilege and my honor henceforth to suffer shame for His dear Name, Who has called me to this high estate. I pray God that I may have grace to stand unmoved amid the strife of tongues, and steadfastly to continue to the end, not far off, in the Apostles' doctrine and fellowship, and the breaking of the bread, and the prayers. The present, in all that is evanescent in sight and sound will soon pass away, and the real issue will abide in bold relief. As we look back, my Brother, upon the fourth and fifth ages of the Church, we do not much occupy ourselves with the wealth of the Eastern Empire or the prowess of the West, we are not dazzled by the splendor of Constantius' Court, or the jewels of Justina, we do not think about, save to pity, the wretched timeserving Bishops, who sold their faith for a temporary flash of this world's glory, for a mere mess of pottage, but we look with the profoundest reverence and thankfulness to God upon the commanding forms of St. Athanasius, in his exile, St. Basil, with his sheepskin, St. Chrysostom, unyielding beneath the frowns and threats of imperial wealth and beauty, and St. Ambrose, counting his life worthless in comparison with fidelity to his divine Master. The evanescent of those days has long since been buried in oblivion, and the real alone remains, the champions of the Catholic faith, and those who set themselves in array against Christ—Christ and antichrist. We see them somewhat as we shall see them in the judgment of God at the end. So now with us the din of voices will soon be hushed, the newspapers with their words of sharp denunciation or sycophantic praise, the frowns, the smiles, the sneers, the personalities will ere long be forgotten, and the entire generation of men now living will die and be buried, but the real issue of this consecration will abide and be measured and understood. In any event it awaits the just judgment of God, and in reference to that awful ordeal I would not for all that creation could bestow shift my position one hair's breadth from that on which I stand, for I hear my Lord asking me, "what is a man profited if he shall gain the whole world and lose his own soul." "So, then, every one of us must give account of himself to God."

GEORGE F. SEYMOUR,
Bishop of Springfield.

SPRINGFIELD, ILL., Sept. 1, 1892.

APPENDICES.

APPENDIX I.

MY CIRCULAR LETTER TO THE BISHOPS.

SPRINGFIELD, ILL., May 16, 1891.

To the Right Reverend..............................

Bishop of..............................

RT. REV. AND DEAR BRO.: We have reached a crisis in the history of our Church.

The Bishops, in my judgment, in the event of the Rev. Dr. Brooks' confirmation as Bishop-elect of Massachusetts, coming before them for approval, will be called upon to answer, each to his God and to the Church, whether he holds and believes—

1. Episcopal ordination as necessary to authorize a man to minister in holy things, and especially to celebrate the Holy Communion or not.

2. The three orders of the Sacred Ministry as of divine appointment or not; and

3. The homoousion ($\accentset{\prime}{o}\mu oo\acute{v}\sigma\iota o\nu$), the essential divinity of our Blessed Lord, to be of *the Faith* (de fide) or not.

How any Bishop of our Communion, with the *vows of his Episcopate* upon him, with the *oath of his consecration* binding him, with the Prayer Book in its services, offices, articles and ordinal before him, and with the terms proposed as a basis of christian unity by the unanimous voice of the House of Bishops committing him, can give a negative answer to these questions, passes my comprehension.

The confirmation and consecration of the Rev. Dr. Brooks, unless he recalls and withdraws his repeated statements, and explains his avowed sympathy with those who disown and repudiate the divinity of our Lord Jesus Christ, I regard as most disastrous to our Branch of the Church of God, since our Episcopate will thus be committed to the position that *the polity* of the Church Catholic, **and the faith** once delivered unto the saints, as touching *its fundamental article* in the creed of Christendom, are matters indifferent.

No one can forecast the horrible consequences which will follow such a position, deliberately taken by the major number of the Bishops as representing our Church.

I feel it to be my duty, under the obligations of my vows as a Bishop in the Church of God, and as bound by my oath, and as fearing the just judgment of God, if I forbear to raise a note of warning to my brethren, to address to them this letter in the confidence of our relation to each other as sharing in the same awful responsibilty of maintaining the faith pure and undefiled, and handing it on as we received it to those who are very soon to succeed us in our trust of the sacred deposit of faith and orders for the sake of all mankind.

With sincere fraternal regard, and in deep anguish of spirit, faithfully yours,

GEORGE F. SEYMOUR,
Bishop of Springfield.

P. S.—Perhaps I ought to add that the Rev. Dr. Brooks is an absolute stranger to me. I have never, to my knowledge, spoken to him, and there is not, in my relation to this question, the slightest admixture of personal feeling. I can truly say that my course would be the same were my father, or brother, or son, or dearest friend to be substituted in this issue for Dr. Brooks. It is a question of loyalty to our Lord, and to His Church; it is a question which touches my own salvation. G. F. S.

APPENDIX II.

LETTERS ADDRESSED BY ME TO THE REV. DR. PHILLIPS BROOKS, WITH A VIEW TO ENABLE ME TO GIVE MY CONSENT TO HIS CONSECRATION, AND HIS REPLIES.

ON THE CARS, IN MOTION, GOING TO
DENVER, COLORADO, May 30, 1891.

Rev. and Dear Bro.:

This note is written by a man to a man. I am personally a stranger to you, but we are of the same household of faith, and are brought into close relation to each other by what may be called an accident in life.

Possibly you and I are both misunderstood, and are so situated that it is almost impossible for us to remove the misapprehension, which prevails, without a sacrifice of self-respect, which we ought not to make, and cannot make.

I am bound by the most sincere conviction of its truth, as well as by oath to uphold the essential divinity of our Blessed Lord enshrined in the ὁμοούσιον of the Nicene Creed. (Note—My ink in fountain pen gives out, and I must use lead pencil, pardon, please, paper and pencil.)

Information reaches me from various sources that you do not accept the Virgin birth of Jesus and the resurrection of His Body, or if you do not go so far yourself, that you maintain that the denial of these Articles of the

Catholic Faith is not inconsistent with a man's taking Holy Orders, or if ordained, remaining in the ministry, and teaching his negations of these verities, while clothed with the authority and acting under the sanction of the Church.

Such assertions, my Brother, are confidently made, and facts are adduced in confirmation, as alleged letters written by you to the Rev. ——— ———, of sympathy with him in his assaults upon Holy Scripture, and the supernatural birth and bodily resurrection of Jesus Christ; your association of yourself with Unitarians in acts of public worship, and assertions of yours in private conversation to the effect that you did not accept the faith in the incarnation of our Lord, as it is believed in by most Christians.

Now I am placed in a most painful position. The Faith is dearer to me than all else, than life itself. I am asked to give my consent to the consecration of one about whom gather clouds of doubt and misgiving as to his soundness in belief touching the truth of truths, as I hold it, and as the Church holds and teaches.

Now, Brother, what am I to do in such a case? What would the State do if there were any question about the loyalty of one of her citizens, whom she was about to honor with the command of a squadron in her navy, or a division of her army? Would she not in some way clear up the doubt before she made the appointment, and would she not be justified in so doing? Nay, would she not on every account be compelled to pursue such a course? Would not the citizen himself welcome such an investigation?

You remember what capital was made in the last Presidential campaign out of an incautious expression of political sympathy by the British Minister.

It adds to the complications of your case that the secular, sectarian and infidel press take very great interest in your confirmation, and hearty friendship and sympathy are professed by those, who in so doing damage your reputation as a Nicene Christian, and injure your cause as a Bishop-elect.

Now, my dear Brother, under these delicate complications and distressing circumstances, what course ought to be pursued?

I have my own view, but it may not be yours, and if I state it, you are in no way committed to adopt it. You may leave this letter unanswered, and I shall feel in no way aggrieved. I recognize the fact that I am intruding upon you, and you may feel annoyed at my apparent presumption.

I may be making a mistake, if so, let me beg of you to believe that it is an error of judgment, not of intention or heart.

I may not be able to put myself in your place, because you may hold views of interpretation of the Bible and formulated statements of doctrine in which I do not share, and hence your relation to the present issue would be modified by such views.

But looking at the question as I do. if doubts had arisen through my own words and conduct, ungenerously construed perhaps. which placed me in a false position, so that I would be misunderstood without explanation, I would in some way strive to set myself right.

You are the better able to do this, because no one could justly suspect or misinterpret your motives.

The Episcopate of Massachusetts could not be an object of ambition to Phillips Brooks. Your integrity of character, your truth and honor are above all price. and with the Ordinal and the Episcopal Oath confronting you in consecration. these are brought into question in the minds of some, I may say of very many.

If I have made a mistake in addressing you, pardon me, dear Brother. If I can in any way serve you. I am ready to do my best loyally and truly.

    Respectfully and faithfully yours,

        GEORGE F. SEYMOUR.

For the REV. PHILLIPS BROOKS, D. D.,

    Boston. Mass.

REPLY OF BISHOP BROOKS TO THE FOREGOING LETTER.

---

    233 CLARENDON ST., BOSTON, June 3, 1891.

Dear Bishop Seymour:

I thank you for the friendliness and courtesy of your note, and I wish very much that I had it in my power to relieve the perplexity in which you find yourself.

But I beg you to think carefully, and see whether it is at all right that I should make special exposition of my faith and justification of my actions under the present circumstances, and with reference to the approaching vote of the Bishops upon my nomination to the Bishopric of Massachusetts.

I have been for thirty-two years a minister of the Church, and I have used her services joyfully and without complaint. I have preached in many places, and with the utmost freedom. I have written and published many volumes, which I have no right to ask anybody to read, but which will give to any one who chooses to read them clear understanding of my way of thinking. My acts have never been concealed.

Under these circumstances, I cannot think it well to make any utterance of faith or pledge of purpose at the present time. Certainly I made none to my brethren here, when they chose me to be their Bishop, and I cannot help thinking that you will think I am right in making none now, when the election is passing to its final stages.

At any rate, I am sure you will believe that my decision in the matter is made not merely in indulgence of my own feelings, but with most serious consideration of what seem to me to be the best interests of the Church which we love.

I must beg you to be assured of this, and to believe me.

Very faithfully and truly yours,

PHILLIPS BROOKS.

My Second Letter to the Rev. Dr. Brooks.

DENVER, COL., June 9, 1891.

Rev. and Dear Brother:

I thank you for your courteous reply to my note.

You will pardon me for drawing your attention to a fundamental distinction, which differentiates your case from any other which has fallen under my observation, and which, I trust, you will so far appreciate as to see in it a justification, from my point of view, for approaching you with my former letter.

In other instances, inferences have been drawn from the associations of men with Church parties, and they have been identified with views and opinions which they may or may not have adopted, and popular clamor and prejudice have been excited against them in consequence.

In your case, the issue raised is not one of Church parties or schools, of high, low or broad. Were such the case you would never have heard from me; you would have had my hearty approval from the outset, as I feel that a Diocese should have its own choice respected in the selection of a chief pastor.

But in your case the question passes beyond Church parties and schools to the *fundamental verity* of the Christian Faith, and the doubts excited were occasioned by alleged acts and words of *your own,* running through several years of your exceptionally brilliant ministry. It is this fact, *and this alone*, which brought me to you, my dear Brother, for explanation, *as you alone* could remove the anxiety.

The ὁμοούσιον of the Nicene Creed, accepted in the ages all along by the Church Catholic, has closed forever the questions touching our Blessed Lord's divinity. No interpretation or practice can be allowed which would deprave the precious doctrine enshrined in that term, or suggest the inference that it was a matter indifferent whether it were maintained as of supreme importance or not.

A Bishop is bound by his oath to protect the faith, and hence you must see, my Brother, the extremely painful and delicate position in which I find myself placed in relation to your confirmation. It is not what *others* have said about you, but what *you* are reported to have said *yourself*, on several occasions, and acts more significant and conclusive than words, which *you*, as it is alleged, have done. *You alone* could remove these doubts, which could not, in my mind have been excited, in the face of your long and faithful ministry, *by any one except yourself*. Hence, as a man and a Bishop, I went directly to you, as the only one who could relieve me from my distress.

This is my justification for my letter to you. I did not see, I do not see, how I could do otherwise, if I wished to reach the truth. I venture to think that you have not appreciated the real bearings of the situation as it presents itself to some of us—at all events, to one who would protect your honor as jealously and sacredly as his own.

I have written on my own responsibility alone, and I may add for myself, that as to the salvation of Christians of other names—of Unitarians and of the heathen—probably my comprehensiveness is as largely inclusive as your own.

Of course, my dear Brother, this note calls for no reply.

Respectfully and sincerely yours,

GEORGE F. SEYMOUR.

For the REV. DR. PHILLIPS BROOKS,
Bishop-elect, Boston, Mass.

---

233 CLARENDON ST., BOSTON, MASS.,
June 13, 1891.

My Dear Bishop Seymour:

I thank you for your letter. Some day we shall meet, I hope, and talk over all this. Meanwhile I must say nothing, except to assure you that I am

Yours sincerely,

PHILLIPS BROOKS.

The RIGHT REVEREND DR. SEYMOUR.

These letters of Bishop Brooks were not written for publication any more than were mine. I could not very well print my own without including his also, and I feel no hesitation in doing so without consulting the Bishop, who is in Europe, and obtaining his consent, because they are in themselves so admirable.

While they do not give me the satisfaction which I sought to obtain, still in another way, they do, and that most emphatically. Doctor, now Bishop Brooks, refers me to his published writings, and his acts, which he says, very truly, were "never concealed," for an explanation of his faith and his administration of the offices and sacraments of the Church. This declaration brings his books and conduct, covering the later years of his ministry, before the public, as his acknowledged exposition of his beliefs and principles of official action as a Presbyter in the Church. It was these sermons and addresses and acts on public occasions which caused my perplexity and distress and sent me to him, their author, for relief.

When it was announced that a majority of the Bishops had consented to his consecration, I felt that Dr. Brooks' status was altered, and that restraints, which had hitherto kept his lips sealed, as he implied in his letter, were removed, and that in consequence, if he were rightly approached, he might now make some statement, which would lessen, if it did not cure the distress which his consecration would occasion thousands of Churchmen throughout the world.

Accordingly I appealed to the Presiding Bishop, who by age and position seemed to me to be the proper person to address Dr. Brooks, and obtain from him, if he could, some such statement.

APPENDIX III.

My Letter to the Presiding Bishop, Urging him to Approach the Rev. Dr. Brooks.

Springfield, Ill., Bishop's House,
August 11, 1891.

Rt. Rev. and Dear Bro.:

Now that the Rev. Dr. Brooks has been confirmed as Bishop-elect by a majority of our Bishops, and order has been taken for his consecration, and publication has been made of the same, the reasons, which from delicacy have hitherto closed his lips, have been removed, and it is now within his choice, with perfect propriety, to relieve himself from the suspicion which *his own acts and words* have brought upon him, and the Church from the damaging consequences which must arise, in case he be consecrated without such explanation.

Whatever you or other Bishops may think, the outside world insists through its press, that the issues settled by the admission of the Rev. Dr. Brooks to the Episcopate, are that the *Polity* and the *Faith* of the Church are matters indifferent henceforth, and that the acknowledgment of Episcopal ordination, as necessary to qualify one to administer the sacraments, and of belief in the essential divinity of our Lord Jesus Christ, are no longer required from those who are to be consecrated Bishops.

Whatever may have been the private opinions of Bishops in days gone by, or may be of Bishops now, the case has never so far occurred, where the repudiation of Episcopacy and the treating the essential verities of the faith of the Gospel, as matters indifferent, have been made the issues on which a man's admission to the Episcopate have turned. *Such is the case now.*

You are the Bishop, as our Metropolitan, who can with the most propriety approach the Rev. Dr. Brooks, in reference to what seems to others as well as myself, due from him to the American Church, in view of what *he has said and done*, and the use which the secular, Roman Catholic, sectarian and infidel press is making of his name, to the injury of our Lord's Kingdom on earth.

I regret to be obliged to intrude upon you again, but conscience and a sense of duty compel me to do so, as a step antecedent to others, which must be taken, in case this fails of its effect.

May God help us and strengthen us to do our duty in this crisis, fearless of consequences to ourselves.

Very faithfully yours,
GEORGE F. SEYMOUR.

For the RT. REV. DR. WILLIAMS,
Presiding Bishop,
Middletown, Conn.

P. S. It is my purpose to send copies of this letter to two or three Bishops of our Church.

To this letter the Presiding Bishop made no reply. Whether he approached the Rev. Dr. Brooks I do not know. Dr. Brooks, however, so far as I am informed, made no sign.

This letter, however, seemed to me to be necessary, in order to bring home to the Bishop of Connecticut his responsibility, as *Presiding Bishop*, and as about *to consecrate* Dr. Brooks, and also as a step properly antecedent to a solemn protest, if I were forced ultimately so to place myself on record.

APPENDIX IV.

PROTEST PRESENTED AND READ IMMEDIATELY BEFORE THE CONSECRATION OF THE REV. DR. BROOKS.

Whereas, the Protestant Episcopal Church in the United States of America has a claim on the allegiance of Catholic believers only on the ground of her claim to be considered a branch of the Catholic Church;

And whereas, the recognition of heresy indirect as well as direct goes far to destroy such claim in the case of any religious body;

And whereas, it is announced by authority that the Rt. Rev. the Presiding Bishop and other Rt. Rev. Rulers of our Church are about to consecrate as Bishop, one who has publicly and definitely repudiated the doctrine of an Apostolic Ministry and by consequence of the Holy Catholic Church as always held by the Church (and proven to be so held, by the invariable practice of ordaining as laymen all ministers of the various Protestant bodies conforming to her), and still further, who has publicly and openly compromised, if not repudiated as indifferent his belief in the doctrine of the ever Blessed Trinity and the homoousion of the Son with the Father as affirmed with the Creed of Christendom, by inviting those, who by open profession and life deny the doctrines of the Trinity and the divinity of Jesus Christ, to receive the Holy Communion, which act has always been held in the Catholic Church as the test of recognition as an orthodox Christian, and is so formally declared by our Church as requiring the recitation of the Apostles' or Nicene Creed as a qualification antecedent to reception, with no abjuration of his errors on the part of such person, thereby giving in some sort recognition to the false doctrines which he maintains;

And whereas, all the Dioceses of the Church are connected together by so close an intercommunion, that what is done by common authority immediately affects them all, and every Bishop, Priest, Deacon and Layman connected with the same.

On these grounds therefore we in our place being Bishops of the Protestant Episcopal Church in the United States of America, by way of relieving our consciences do hereby solemnly protest against said consecration and disown it as removing our Church from its present ground and tending to her disorganization unless the said Bishop-elect shall before the consecration abjure and disavow his false teaching and practice.

GEORGE F. SEYMOUR,
Bishop of Springfield.

(Signed by two Bishops.)

NOTE.—Doubtless more Bishops would have signed had I been allowed by the Assessor of the Presiding Bishop to learn what Bishops declined to consent. This information was refused on my application for it as a Bishop. In such a crisis I wished to consult my Brethren, who agreed with me as to the consecration, as to what was best to be done. This state of things ought not to be permitted to continue. G. F. S.

APPENDIX V.

Unitarian Baptism: Damaging Commendations.

In this connection I desire to submit facts and samples of testimony, which conclusively prove that our Church, the faithful everywhere, had reason to expect, nay, had a right to demand that the chief Pastors of the flock would require some explanation or retraction touching his past life and conduct as a clergyman before they admitted the Bishop-elect to the Episcopal office.

1. His status as a baptized man is open to serious doubt, as the service was performed, it is alleged and never denied, by *a Unitarian Minister*, and waiving the issue of the validity of lay baptism, there is a question whether the element of water was used, and still further whether the form of words prescribed by our Lord was employed. The Bishop-elect, when approached upon the subject, I am told, absolutely refused to submit to hypothetical baptism with a view to cure any doubts, which might exist, and to allay and set at rest the painful misgivings of thousands of his fellow churchmen.

2. "A man is known by the company which he keeps," is a trite saying, which embodies a recognized truth. It was the

principle which this proverb implies which led to the excitement which prevailed at the time the present Bishop of London was advanced to the See of Exeter. In Bishop Temple's case there was nothing to excite or justify suspicion from his own past life or acts or words, all was based, or seemed to be based upon the single fact that he was in bad company with his innocent essay in the volume, which was censured by the Convocation of the Province of Canterbury. What then is to be said of a case where the Bishop-elect's associations have been in his official life very largely and conspicuously with those, who refuse the Church's polity, deny her creed and disown and oppose her order, and whole system? Yet such has been notoriously the case with the present Bishop of Massachusetts through a period of many years, if current public testimony is to be credited, and no denial or attempt at explanation has ever been made, so far as I know, or have reason to believe. Prior to his confirmation the secular press was extensively and persistently employed by the friends of the Bishop-elect to promote his interests.

In order to exhibit the character of his company, the sort of men, who were anxious that Dr. Brooks should be made a Bishop in the Church of God, I submit the following poetic tribute to his praise, and the headlines, which condense the spirit of the testimony of the ministers of several denominations, which fills several of the columns of the Boston Herald of June 3d, 1891, and the Boston Daily Advertiser of October 13, 1891.

The Boston Herald, Wednesday, June 3d, 1891, presents the following summary of testimony in favor of the Bishop elect:

"All Pay him Honor.—Clerical Views of Dr. Brooks' election.—Various Boston divines give their opinions.—As a Bishop he would do much for Christianity.—Praise for his noble piety and great gifts.—His choice an honor to the Episcopal Church."—"Unitarians would welcome Dr. Brooks' confirmation as Bishop."—"Methodist clergy hail Dr. Brooks' election as a wise step."—"Baptist opinion— The Episcopal office will limit his power for usefulness." "Grand thing for Christianity.—Universalist divines think the Episcopal Church has honored itself." "His piety broad and noble.—Influence to which a Congregationalist attributes his election."—"A Presbyterian view—Defeat would be a set back to the best Christian America can offer."

The Boston Advertiser of Tuesday, October 13th, 1891, has the following headlines over several columns of testimony, and the sonnet, which I submit in full:

"Phillips Brooks—The man, the preacher, the Bishop-elect. Tributes from his brother clergymen in Boston—Admiration, respect and affection are mingled.—No office can add to his present station.—Fervent words from the Rev. Drs. Griffis, Horton, Savage, Lorrimer, Rexford, Little, Haynes, Horr, Herrick, and many others."—"Heber Newton's plea.—He wants Episcopal Bishops to be leaders, and is greatly encouraged by Dr. Brooks' election." The sonnet follows:

> "God said. 'I make a man;' and lo the creeds
> Broke in his hands as did the withes that bound
> The Hebrew giant! Not that he was found
> Careless of words, but that all human needs
> Plead with him saying, 'Christlike he who heeds
> Man's want and sorrow, putting these above
> All forms and phrases in the name of love:
> For words are mockery when the time wants deeds?'
> And in this spirit, lo, the man became
> Greater than creeds or office; and all these
> He used for ends that make success and fame
> Seem petty as pass by God's centuries.
> And so, as truth and love transcend all books,
> The man transcends the Bishop, Phillips Brooks.'"

Oct. 12, 1891.   M. J. SAVAGE.

No one, I am sure, wishes to abridge, abate, or withdraw one single word of praise which Bishop Brooks receives for his gifts natural and acquired, or for his excellencies of character, but when commendation comes to a man from the antagonists of the principles, which he has deliberately accepted and over and over again bound himself by solemn vow and promise to teach and uphold on the ground of his liberality in compromising those principles with those who refuse them and despise them, the feeling is very different. Socially we are not at war with Unitarians, Congregationalists, Methodists and Baptists, but as regards the faith, and polity, and administration of God's Church, as set forth in our Book of Common Prayer in its creeds, offices, articles, and ordinal, we are at issue with them, and we cannot compromise our principles by speaking and acting as though their denial of our position was as truly right as our affirmation; an affirmation, be it observed, to which we are bound by written obligation in the formularies of our Church, and our assent thereto by pledge, and promise, and vow under the most solemn sanctions known to mankind. The question is not one of social relation, or civil recognition, or kindly intercourse in the walks of daily life, but it is an issue of fidelity, as it seems to me, to honor and truth.

Were we at war with several foreign nations for causes universally understood, it might be considered a little discouraging, if one, who was nominated as a general in our army, was urged upon those in authority for confirmation with unanimous voice by our foes, and with the plea that he was just the man for the place, because he habitually made light of the issues at stake, or treated them as matters of supreme indifference, and was ready to concede everything to them, our public enemies. It would be more than discouraging if it were found that those with whom the responsibility rested of giving or withholding appointment yielded apparently to the pressure, and said, after the case was fully presented to them, "it is our pleasure to give him a share of the command of our armies. Let him be one of our generals." The exhibit presented above is sad beyond expression to those who hold as a religious belief what the Church teaches in her creed, her ordinal, her offices and her articles. Two plus two cannot be three and four and five. They are four, and he who says it is a matter indifferent whether you reckon the amount as three or four or five, is a traitor to mathematical truth. The doctrine of the Trinity and its denial, the polity of the Church as set forth in the Ordinal, and its repudiation, the natural depravity of man, as taught by the Baptismal Office, and the Catechism, and the Articles, and the antagonistic view, these opposite teachings cannot be held by the same persons at the same time as truths. It is impossible for them to tolerate each other. To play fast and loose with the doctrine of the Trinity and the threefold ministry and original sin, to act and speak as though they were matters indifferent whether one held them as truths, or rejected them as errors will do for an infidel, but it will not do for a deacon, priest or bishop in the Church of God. He is under bonds to hold them and teach them. He obtained his status as a Minister of Christ in the Church by making the pledge that he would hold and teach them. They are central fundamental principles in the economy of the Church, and cannot be regarded as secondary matters, or matters indifferent. He cannot escape by asserting that he considers them as non-essential, since their relative importance is not left for him to decide. The Church pronounces them to be fundamental, and exacts this acknowledgment from every one whom she admits to teach under her authority and in her name. He therefore, who repudiates this obligation judges himself, and mankind will judge him. The shouts of praise, and the din of laudatory voices may seem for a time to prevail, but the silent thought of the breast as it grasps the relation of such a man to the Book of Common Prayer, and his obligations as a clergyman and his oath as a Bishop, anticipates in condemnation the just judgment of God.

APPENDIX VI.

PELAGIANISM.

The Bishop of Massachusetts seems to be, as far as I can gather from his public utterances, a Pelagian. Pelagianism I need not say is directly in conflict with the teaching of Holy Scripture and of the Church. St. Augustine's Antipelagian writings have made Western Christendom familiar with the heresy and supply its antidote. Pelagianism is absolutely irreconcilable with the teaching of our Book of Common Prayer. The following passage represents much of the teaching of the Bishop of Massachusetts, which I have read. It embodies its spirit. In a volume entitled "Twenty Sermons." New York. 1890. Sermon 3d. p. 46, occurs this statement. "I cannot think, I will not think about the Christian Church as if it were a selection out of humanity. In its idea it is humanity. The hard, iron faced man, whom I meet upon the street, the degraded sad faced man, who goes to prison, the weak silly faced man, who haunts society, the discouraged, sad faced man, who drags the chain of drudgery, they are all members of the Church, members of Christ, children of God, heirs of the kingdom of heaven. Their birth made them so. Their baptism declared the truth, which their birth made true. It is impossible to estimate their lives aright, unless we give this truth concerning them the first importance.

1. The writer seems to have made up his mind upon this subject, and avows his belief as a fixed and unalterable conviction. "I cannot think," he says, "*I will not think.*" This assertion reminds one of St. Thomas in his state of doubt when he declares, "Except I shall see in His hands the print of the nails, etc., *I will not believe.*" St. John xx 25.)

2. His view of the Church flatly contradicts our Lord's description of the Church in the name which He gives to it, "ecclesia," "a selection." "On this rock," He says, "I will build My Church (ecclesia) and the gates of hell, etc.," (St. Matt. xvi 18) and in His teaching respecting it directly and by parable. One becomes accustomed to what is shocking to the moral and religious sense. I remember on one occasion being filled with horror, when a woman no longer young, and thoroughly hardened in her prejudices, was conversing with me, and raising objections to the use of unleavened bread in the Holy Eucharist. I sought to answer her arguments and satisfy her doubts, and finally I told her that it amounted almost to a demonstration, as we read the Gospel narrative that our Saviour instituted the sacrament in the use of unleavened bread. "Well!" said she in reply, "if He did, He was wrong." I left her house in consternation. I was fearful lest it might fall upon me. Alas! Now a school of teaching has crept into the church which does not hesitate to assert that our Lord, as touching his humanity, is full of errors. No far reaching analysis is needed to bring this awful impiety face to face with bald

Nestorianism. It involves a denial of the hypostatic union of the two perfect natures in the one divine Person, and resolves the natures into two independent personalities. Alas! that one should be admitted into the Episcopal office by the suffrages of my brethren, not by the edict of the state, who seems flatly and directly to contradict the adorable Lord Himself.

The Bishop of Massachusetts asserts that birth makes men members of Christ, children of God and heirs of the kingdom of heaven, and that baptism simply proclaims as true what birth has already made true.

Need I remind any one who is at all acquainted with the Book of Common Prayer that such teaching is in manifest conflict with its letter and its spirit throughout? Do we need examples of the contradiction? The Bishop of Massachusetts says men are made members of Christ, etc., by natural birth. The Catechism teaches the child to say in answer to the question "Who gave you this name? My sponsors in Baptism; wherein I was made a member of Christ, the child of God and an inheritor of the kingdom of heaven."

Again in the office of Baptism the minister addresses the congregation and beseeches them "to call upon God the Father, through our Lord Jesus Christ, that of His bounteous goodness He will grant to the candidates for Baptism *that which by nature they cannot have*; that they may be baptized with water and the Holy Ghost, and received into Christ's holy Church, and be made lively members of the same." In the Confirmation office the Bishop in his prayer to God says, as taught by the Church, "Almighty and everlasting God who hast vouchsafed to regenerate these Thy servants by water and the Holy Ghost, etc." Article IX affirms "original sin standeth not in the following of Adam, (as the Pelagians do vainly talk) but it is the fault and corruption of every man that naturally is engendered of the offspring of Adam, whereby man is very far gone from original righteousness, and is of his own nature inclined to evil, so that the flesh lusteth always contrary to the spirit, and therefore in every person born into this world it deserveth God's wrath and damnation." The Psalmist declares (Psalm 51st 5) "Behold I was shapen in wickedness and in sin hath my mother conceived me." Is it necessary to multiply quotations from God's word and the Prayer Book?

I am quite well aware that such teaching as the above has not been unknown in our communion. Notably we find it in a sermon of the brilliant and tenderhearted Rev. Frederick W. Robertson of the English Church. The influence of the author is deservedly so great, that it is worth while to say a few words to expose the error into which he unwittingly fell. Robertson claims that the view, which makes Baptism the new or second birth, reduces the sacrament to "magic." He forgets that Christ, the Eternal Son of God, is behind the sacraments; men, possibly devils, are behind magic. He forgets that to refuse the sacraments of the Gospel as means of grace, because they involve the employment of a material agent is to reject the miracles of our Lord for the same reason. To say that the Catholic doctrine of the sacraments is "materialism of the grossest kind" is of necessity to make the same charge against the incarnation of Jesus Christ, since in the taking flesh, God employed matter as the instrument whereby He revealed Himself to mankind, and became the Saviour of the race by shedding His precious blood upon the cross. The Eternal "Word was made FLESH, and dwelt among us." (St. John, i: 14.) is the statement which announces the law of the incarnation, the employment of matter as an instrument by the infinite God to confer the greatest of all blessings even Himself as part and parcel of humanity upon mankind. The law of the Head is the law of the members, the law of Christ incarnate is the law of His Church, His Body. He was behind His miracles. He is behind His sacraments. In both cases alike He employs material agencies, water-pots full of water, clay and spittle, the spoken word in the former, miracles; water, bread and wine in the latter, sacraments. There is no more materialism in the one case than in the other. To say that the sacraments as interpreted by the Church Catholic are magic, and that the miracles are not, is to confuse thought, and impose (of course not intentionally) upon the people with specious sophistry. Let me say that it would be worth the while of these persons, who are always crying out "materialistic, gross materialism," to name a single blessing which man has ever enjoyed, or does enjoy in this life, which does not come to him through the agency of matter. There may be such, but as yet I do not know of any. The greatest, highest blessing, Jesus Christ, comes to me through matter, and the lowest, in the sphere of the supply of mere bodily wants, comes to me through matter, and all, so far as I know that lie between, come to me along the same path; matter is employed in their conveyance by Him "from Whom cometh every good and perfect gift."

The illustration which the gentle and affectionate Robertson gave to enforce his view of Baptism is entirely misleading, unquestionably it deceived him. He likens the candidate for Holy Baptism to the heir to the throne, and urges that as coronation is said to crown or make the King or Queen, although it simply proclaims a fact which was already a fact, so baptism simply solemnly publishes a truth, which was already made a truth by nature. The illustration is specious, but it is utterly fallacious. In the first place it is not said either legally or historically that coronation makes the sovereign. Reigns are not dated from the act of coronation, but from the accession. In the next place the cases are not parallel, they are separated by the very question in dispute between Pelagius and the Catholic Church. The English constitution designates the heir to the throne by criteria, which natural birth alone can meet, and hence natural birth makes the sovereign, presumptively while he is the Heir Apparent, and actually, the moment his predecessor dies.

God's Constitution, the Bible, reveals man's state by nature, and the authorized interpreter of Holy Scripture, the Catholic Church, not only fails to find in it that man is by natural birth the heir of the kingdom of heaven, but teaches just the contrary, when she says in her Catechism in response to the question, "What is the inward and spiritual grace of Baptism?" "A death unto sin, and a new birth unto righteousness: *for being by nature born in sin and the children of wrath, we are hereby made the children of grace."* The Rev. F. W. Robertson and those who agree with him may be right on this point with Pelagius, but their position is not tenable in the Catholic Church, if she speaks her mind in the General Councils, and the authoritative teaching of her formularies.

Pelagius taught or is held responsible for teaching, that the incarnation, our Lord's birth into this world, conferred divine sonship upon all mankind alike, made all men *actually* "the children of God, members of Christ, and heirs of the kingdom of heaven." The Church teaches that the incarnation makes it possible for all men to be saved, puts it within their power to become by regeneration the children of God, members of Christ, and heirs of the kingdom of heaven. Here again the issue is, not whether Pelagius and those who accept his teaching are right or wrong, but whether as holding what the Church rejects and condemns they have a moral right to represent her at the font and the altar, in the pulpit and the bishop's chair.

The question is whether a man who has twice signed the following declaration just before he was admitted to the Diaconate, and just before he was admitted to the Presbyterate, and practically repudiated it throughout his entire ministry of many years, in word and deed, and published utterances will be likely to keep the same declaration on his admission to the Episcopate, even though that declaration be thrown into the form of a promise of conformity, and be required of him under the sanction of an oath.

This is the declaration required by the 7th Article of the Constitution of our Church to be subscribed by every person, who is admitted to Holy Orders. "I do believe the Holy Scriptures of the Old and New Testament to be the Word of God, and to contain all things necessary to salvation, and I do solemnly engage to conform to the Doctrines and Worship of the Protestant Episcopal Church in the United States."

This seems to be explicit enough and solemn enough to bind the conscience of any one in a normal moral condition. But when one comes to be consecrated a Bishop the same declaration substantially is required of him as a promise of conformity to the Doctrine, Discipline, and Worship of the Protestant Episcopal Church, uttered by him in the hearing of the congregation, and standing before the altar of his God. The promise is exacted under the sanction of an oath, and is as follows: "In the name of God, Amen. I ———, chosen Bishop of the Protestant Episcopal Church in ———, do promise conformity and obedience to the Doctrine, Discipline, and Worship of the Protestant Episcopal Church in the United States of America. So help me God through Jesus Christ."

The excuse made for the man who has exercised the lower ministries of the Church in notorious violation of his twice signed declaration, when he is urged upon the Church for a share in the highest ministry, and he comes to repeat his declaration in the form of a public verbal promise, and under the sanction of an oath, the excuse is made for him when apprehension is expressed that the same anomia will be exhibited by him in the Episcopate as in the Presbyterate, and that he will be as reckless of the obligation of his

Bishop's oath, as he was and continued to be of the declaration, which held him by his own signature twice affixed, "O, he means well, he cannot understand theological distinctions, and hence he contradicts the Church in his teaching and conduct without knowing that he is doing so." This might be an excuse to be urged in palliation of his guilt, if he were convicted of heresy, but we ask is such a statement to be accepted as a reason for allowing a man to be promoted, when it is known that in accordance with the safe-guards, which the Church hath interposed to protect her from false teachers he ought to be kept out? Would such a course be pursued in admitting surgeons to hospitals, lawyers to the bench, pharmacists to drug stores, engineers to take charge of engines? Would natural defect be pleaded in any of these or like cases as a reason why incompetency should be discounted or disregarded altogether and a man allowed to take charge of interests, which he was by nature disqualified from administering? Never. Men are too careful of their precious lives and worldly interests to run such risks for a single instant. What are we to say then of Bishops, who have in their custody the eternal interests of mankind? Of course the reply may be made that the Bishops, who said "aye" are satisfied in their own minds that the teaching of the one whom they confirm is as good if not better than that of the Church of God. When this explanation is accepted, it follows that the Episcopate of the Church in the United States by a majority of their votes declare that the faith and discipline of the Church as embodied in her creed, offices, articles, constitution and canons are matters indifferent, which anyone may hold or repudiate as he pleases. Observe I am not speaking of issues which divide the members of the church into schools or parties, but of questions which mark off the Church from infidelity, agnosticism and atheism.

APPENDIX VII.

ARIANISM.

The revelation made by the following letters is sad in the extreme, and force me to ask and press home the question, what do my brother Bishops mean, who gave their consent to the consecration of the Bishop of Massachusetts without any public explanation or retraction on his part?

Am I to understand that in their judgment a practical denial of the essential divinity of the Person of Jesus Christ is no longer a bar to admission to the Episcopal office? If their affirmative votes "let him be a Bishop" mean anything, they mean just that.

The letters which follow disclose a state of things which fills me with dismay. It would seem that the Rector of Trinity Church, Boston, had been in the habit of giving a general invitation in some way of his own devising, to the congregation to receive the Holy Communion, over and above the forms which convey the Church's invitation, and that Unitarians, *known to be such, were accustomed to commune in Trinity Church*, and members of Trinity Church often communed in Unitarian Churches. Now, consider what these facts compel us to conclude:

First. That the Rector of Trinity Church, Boston, did not, and, so far as we know, does not now believe that in Personality, our Lord Jesus Christ is very and eternal God, of one substance with the Father, eternal in being. since this article of the faith the Unitarian denies. It matters not where he places the Saviour, whether at the apex of creation, or on a level with mankind, the interval between the highest and the lowest grade of creation, is as nothing compared to the infinite abyss between the uncreated and the created. and the Arian of whatever type sinks the eternal Son of God by an infinite degradation from the uncreated essence of the Divine Personality to the condition of created life. It is inconceivable to me that any one, who holds the essential divinity of our Saviour, could expose Him to such intolerable insult, and that too in violation of ordination vows and the law of the Church universal, and the whole structure and spirit of the liturgy, and the creed, placed as a bar to protect the sacrament from such profanation. He who does this thing must be himself an Arian. Charity constrains one to resort to this explanation.

On the other hand, in the view of the Unitarian. he who believes that our Lord is the very and eternal God, and pays Him, as he must. the honor due to His divinity, *is an idolater.* How, then, can the Unitarian admit him to his assemblies, and allow him to join with him in his most solemn service and most sacred act? The Apostle asks, and I ask, "What part hath he that believeth with an infidel? And what agreement hath the temple of God with idols? (2 Cor. vi:15-16).

Second. It appears on the occasion of the consecration of Trinity Church, Boston, in 1877, on the testimony of the Rev, Dr. E. E. Hale, Dr. Brooks was responsible for the invitation given to him and other Unitarian ministers to remain and receive the Holy Communion, and he explains by a special message why what appears to have been his usual unauthorized and personal invitation was not extended.

It is to be regretted that the attempt has been made to throw the responsibility of this transaction upon one who is dead. Even if it were true that Bishop Paddock did in some way seek to break the force of the righteous indignation and distress, which were felt in consequence of the champions of heresy, as the Church accounts heresy, being publicly received as *such to the Holy Communion*, still, so far as it appears, the invitation did not come from him, but on this occasion by a special messenger from the Rector. Moreover, this receiving Unitarians to the Holy Communion was not an exception to the practice of the Rector of Trinity Church, Boston, it was his habitual practice, and, so far as we know, is still.

Third. The Rev. Dr. E. E. Hale is in error about the case of the Rev. Vance Smith being invited by the Archbishop of Canterbury to receive the Holy Communion. This was not the case at all. Directly the reverse was the fact, as the following succinct and emphatic statement of the Archbishop proves:

Letter of the Archbishop to Canon Carter, relative to the case of the Rev. Vance Smith:

"I confess that I do not understand the frame of mind that would lead a teacher of religion to protest against the Nicene Creed, and at the same time to join in a solemn service of which that Creed and its doctrines form from the beginning to the end so prominent a part. Neither can I understand any one feeling it right to invite to our Communion Service a teacher of the Unitarian body which so protests." Life of Archbishop Tait, Vol. 2, p. 70.

With these sentiments of the late Archbishop Tait, I am in full and hearty accord.

It must be recollected, too, that in the first instance even the Dean of Westminister, Dr. Stanley, was not responsible for the Rev. Vance Smith's communicating in the Abbey beyond allowing its use for the purpose of a celebration by the Company of revisers. This Company included, of course, the Rev. Vance Smith, and the invitation went to him as to every other member to attend. He was thrown upon his own responsibility, and the Archbishop very justly criticises his conduct in meeting that responsibility. It is true Dean Stanley espaused the cause of the Rev. Vance Smith, and the judgment of the Upper House of Convocation of the Province of Canterbury was pronounced in a resolution passed by a vote of 10 to 4, on the question of his presence among the revisers, as follows:

"That it is the judgment of this House that no person who denies the Godhead of our Lord Jesus Christ, ought to be invited to join either Company to which is committed the revision of the Authorized Version of Holy Scripture, and that any such person now on either Company should cease to act therewith."

Fourth. With the view, which the Rev. Dr. E. E. Hale takes of the Lord's Supper, and his illustration of a feast

—6

given by the City of Boston, I have nothing to do. He
has a perfect right to hold such opinions, and I am ready
to protect him in the exercise of that right. But it must
be manifest to all that such a view is absolutely and hope-
lessly irreconcilable with the teaching of the Book of Common Prayer and the Ancient Liturgies.

You cannot, with any scheme of comprehension, without
doing violence to reason, and honesty and the moral
sense, bring together and unite in the worship of God the
Unitarian and the Trinitarian. The point at issue involves
the truth of truths, the verity of verities, the doctrine of
doctrines. In the view of the Unitarian, he who acknowl-
edges the Son to be of the same substance with the Father,
and consequently possessing all the attributes of the Father,
and who worships Him as God, *must be an idolater.* The
Rev. Dr. E. E. Hale must regard me as such, his doing so
is an inevitable logical consequence of his estimate of our
Lord, he cannot help it, and I do not find the least fault
for his so thinking of me. I should cease to respect him, if
he treated the fundamental verity of religion *as a matter
of supreme indifference.*

On the other hand the Trinitarian must, as a logical
necessity, regard the Unitarian, in so far as he fails to
acknowledge the Catholic Faith, *as an unbeliever.* It is
impossible that it should or could be otherwise. I beg to
say, therefore, in all that I have written or may write, I
do not mean to be understood as expressing the slightest
feeling of disrespect or unkindness. I see how I must appear in their eyes, I know how they appear in mine. The
only parties with whom I must part company are those

who are false to their principles and their duty as embodied in the vows, which bind them, and the laws which they have sworn to obey. When one thinks of such men he responds with all his heart to the sentiment of old Homer, when the race was young and its sensitiveness to truth was not blunted by many inventions, which men have found out in their ingenious "interpretations."

> "Who dares think one thing and another tell,
> My soul detests him as the gates of hell."

What is the present age mad upon doing? To comprehend and reconcile irreconcilables, to unite and wed incompatibilities, and what will be the net result? The loss of truth, the depraving of the moral sense, the degradation of manhood. Let us see. Here is a man who holds the truth, but he holds it with a feeble grasp. He will not suffer for it, and he is ready to barter it for a price. He knows that two plus two make four. This is the truth. On his right is one who affirms that two plus two make *five*, and on his left is one who urges two plus two make *three*. He knows full well that two plus two do not make either five or three, but the age demands *charity*, as it calls falsehood and dishonesty, and so there comes a clever logician with a scheme of comprehension and his proposition is that two plus two make an amount not less than three nor more than five, and then they all sit down in a symposium of love and agreement, and henceforth arithmetic is taught on this basis. What a harvest of good fruits this comprehensive unity in the realm of figures would produce in the world of business.

So in the sphere of Christianity, break down the metes
and bounds of truth, make everything from the being of
God to the condition of man and the terms of redemption
matters of indifference, let them stand for three or four, or
five as you please, so long as you are good natured and
are liberal and popular. What is left? Nothing. Nothing,
the incarnate God is gone, and His Church and salvation.
Forbid it Almighty God.

[From the Christian Register, Boston, Saturday, March 17, 1877.]

THE COMMUNION SERVICE.

To the Editor of the Christian Register:

"I happened to be one of many Unitarians who partook
of the Lord's Supper at Trinity church on the day of dedication. It seemed to me a personal matter, and a very
simple matter, by no means worthy of the attention which
the press has given to it. There is probably always a considerable number of Unitarians who partake of the Lord's
Supper whenever it is administered at Trinity Church; and,
on the other hand, it is probable that many Episcopalians
partake of it whenever it is administered in any large
Unitarian church in this city.

Neither the Unitarian Church nor the Episcopal Church
has ever been coy or narrow in its invitations to it, and,
in practice each church expects and wishes that all who
profess and call themselves Christians shall receive it.

It happens, however, that the narrowness expressed in
that absurd and contradictory phrase "close communion"
has so far affected the general sentiment, that the fact that

thirty or forty clergymen, not Episcopalians, should join in the service on the day of dedication excited some public comment. It would be a pity if any discussion on the subject should confuse any persons who are unwilling to make the communion service the emblem of disunion; and it seems worth while, therefore, to state the principle on which the Episcopal and Unitarian churches give their broad invitation, and on which, whether they gave it or not, it is fitting that Christian men and women should habitually join in the service.

The central principle is that this is the Lord's Supper. It is not Bishop Paddock's supper; it is not Mr. Phillips Brooks' supper; it is Jesus Christ's table, spread for any person who cares for him enough to wish to attend.

If the city of Boston announced that, on a certain day, it would serve an entertainment for all the people in Boston, on the Common, and I wished to attend at that entertainment, being, as I am, one of those people, I should attend. I should not ask the mayor if I was on his list, or the chief of police if I was on his. Having been invited, I should go, and where I found a vacant seat I should sit down. True, I was early taught, on high authority, "never to quarrel with a porter;" and if an ignorant policeman came to me, and ordered me out I might very possibly go away, rather than have a personal altercation with him on an occasion of festivity.

But this is only as a gentleman, because he is a gentleman, often "abates something of his right." I have an entire right to stay—and my staying is the thing of course; my going away would be accidental or exceptional.

In fact, I am a minister of the gospel, and it has been my pleasure to receive thousands of persons to their first communion. I dare not say how often I have told such young persons what I suppose to be the statement wellnigh universal of the church, that they are to receive the Lord's supper wherever they find it administered, "asking no questions for conscience sake." In particular, then, there is no reason why they should ask the officiating clergyman whether they are to partake or no. For, if he is a true man, he knows that he is simply the waiter on the Lord's table on that occasion, sufficiently honored indeed that he is permitted to stand and wait at such a service. It is Jesus Christ who gave the invitation, and gave it to all of us; to Thomas who doubted; to Peter who disowned; and very likely to Judas, who betrayed.

He asked me, though he never commanded me, to join in this service when I met with other people who were joining in it. With that request of his, it is a profound pleasure for me to comply, whenever I meet together with such people.

The true advice to be given to any communicant is to join with the Greek church, with the Roman church, though it be the first of schismatics; with the Episcopal church, though with us it stands in the attitude in which a dissenting church in England stands toward that establishment, which is all rooted in with English institutions.

He will join in the communion with a Presbyterian church, not annoyed that more or less is said about persons in regular standing; or, in one word, where the Lord's table is spread, he will remember who invited him to it.

In reference to the communion at Trinity Church, more or less has been said of Mr. Brooks's invitation to the clergymen present. It is perfectly true that one of the Wardens came to the several pews in which the invited clergy, who were not Episcopalians, sat, and said it was the hope of the minister that they would remain. He said the congregation at large was not solicited to remain from the simple imposibility of administering the communion at one time to so many. This was a perfectly fit reason for Mr. Brooks's courtesy, which otherwise would have been quite unnecessary. The invitation was given eighteen hundred years ago.

As to the attendance of Unitarians at the supper when administered by the Church of England, there is no question whatever as to the practice; and the practice in that Church has great weight in determining the practice of the Protestant Episcopal Church in America.

The service in which Mr. Vance [Smith] partook of the communion with the other translators is well remembered. But it is idle to rest on an incidental practice, where the origin and principle of the whole service indicate what is the true course for those who are in sympathy with it."

E. E. HALE.

[From the Boston Commonwealth, January 30, 1892, p. 5.]

DR. PADDOCK, DR. BROOKS, AND DR. SHATTUCK.

"*To the Editors of the Commonwealth:*

"GENTLEMEN—My attention has been called to a letter in the Guardian, an Episcopal paper published in London. It contains a communication from Mr. G. C. Shattuck, a member of the Standing Committee of the Diocese of Massachusetts, with reference to the charge of admitting Unitarians to the Holy Communion, often made against Dr. Brooks, recently elected Bishop of Massachusetts: (Dr. Shattuck writes as follows.)

"Trinity Church in Boston was consecrated more than fourteen years ago. On that occasion some Unitarian clergymen received the sacrament, and the attention of Dr. Paddock (at that time Bishop) was called to the fact within a few days of the occurrence. The Bishop replied that he alone was responsible for the service, Dr. Brooks, the Rector, having no responsibility. It has always been the custom in Massachusetts to adminnister the Communion to unknown persons applying for it, they assuming their own responsibility. Neither the Bishop nor his assistants in administering the Communion recognized any applying for the Sacrament as Unitarians. Will you allow me to add, that there is hardly a Bishop in this whole country who enjoys to so great an extent the respect and admiration of both his clergy and laity as the present Bishop of Massachusetts."

I am one of the clergymen referred to; and as my name and that of Dr. J. Freeman Clarke have in this connection been alluded to in print, it is proper that I should publicly refer to Dr. Shattuck's letter—which Dr. Paddock would not have printed, were he living.

The transaction was in the highest degree courteous and creditable to the clergy of the Episcopal Church.

Dr. Clarke privately asked me if I should partake of the Communion "if we were not asked". I said to him privately, that I received my invitation eighteen centuries and a half ago and should partake, unless I were asked not to. He said he should also. A few minutes after, a gentleman, personally known to us both, came to each of us, to say that it was the wish of the gentlemen who had the service in charge that all the clergymen present should partake; that the number of persons present was so large that the usual general invitation could not be given, but that it was hoped that all the clergy would unite in the service. We did so, accordingly not as "unknown persons applying for it," but as persons well known to the Bishop and his clergy. We were, in fact, present only because invited. Special seats were provided for us. Neither Bishop Paddock nor the Vestry of Trinity Church would have invited us to the first half of the ceremony, if they had not expected us to join in the whole.

In truth, as Bishop Paddock undoubtedly remembered, the whole principle was settled for the Episcopal Church, when Archbishop Tait invited to the Special Communion, when the revision was begun, Dr. Vance Smith, who sat on the board as the representative of the Unitarian Church of England." Respectfully yours,

EDWARD E. HALE.

South Congregational Church, Boston, Jan. 27, 1892.

THE REV. JAMES FREEMAN CLARKE'S TESTIMONY.

[From the Christian Register, March 10, 1877.]

"As I was one of the liberals who accepted *the personal invitation of Phillips Brooks* to stay to the Communion, I will venture to ask the following question, etc., etc." The italics are mine.

Again in the same letter the Rev. Mr. Clarke writes as follows: "I do not then consider that the brethren who, with myself, gladly stood for a moment in communion with Phillips Brooks and his friends on this occasion sacrificed any principle in so doing. My face was toward the light, for I saw in this act of my friend a faint gleam of the rosy dawn of universal brotherhood which is to come.

" * * * *Phillips Brooks and I were moving in the same direction,* for we were both moving toward *a ground of higher union of spirit* in which all differences of the letter disappear." Italics mine.

Why, I may ask, has Bishop Brooks both before and since his consecration allowed his friends to deny that he ever invited Unitarians and Unitarian ministers *as such* to come to the Holy Communion when he knew that they were placing themselves in a false position and misleading others? Why should Bishop Doane, who had better facilities for knowing the facts than most bishops, if not most people, treat this fact in a letter to an English newspaper as though it were in doubt, an allegation?

APPENDIX VIII.

APOSTOLICAL SUCCESSION.

The issue made is not as to the truth or falsehood of the theory, but whether a man who accepts Holy Orders in the Church is at liberty to repudiate it. I am not discussing the subject of apostolical succession on its merits as to its truth, but I am insisting that the Church, the Protestant Episcopal Church of these United States, lays down the doctrine of apostolical succession as the foundation principle of her Ordinal, and applies it in her practice exclusively in admitting men to her ministry as Deacons, Priests and Bishops.

It is scarcely necessary to adduce specific evidence to prove that the Bishop of Massachusetts, while a Presbyter, repudiated the doctrine of Apostolical Succession, and the ministry as constituted in three orders as taught by the Ordinal.

Aside from Bishop Brooks' intrinsic merits, which have given him so wide a reputation for eloquence and learning, no one cause has contributed more to make him the idol of the people than his attitude towards the Church of which he was and is a minister. He has treated with scorn and proud contempt her ordinal, her offices, her rubrics, her canons and the spirit of divine worship as embodied in her Book of

Common Prayer. This attitude on the part of one so conspicuous in himself fascinated the crowd. The position is so unique for one, who is in a system by his own choice, and yet in word and deed repudiates it, whose sympathies are outside of his home, rather than within it, and whose following is largely made up of the foes of the Church, or of those who are indifferent to her claims, that it attracts attention, and with a vast unthinking multitude it pleases. The popular delusion is that this is liberality. The cry goes up, "the liberal soul deviseth liberal things." It needs not very much reflection to see that this is not liberality, it is disloyalty to vows and promises, to what the system of which the man who acts in this way is a teacher and administrator proposes to him as truth and which he has accepted as truth. Mind, I am not saying that it is truth, but that he has accepted it as truth, and stands before the public as its accredited Ambassador. I am prepared to hear it said, "other men have done the same, and their names are illustrious." This may be, but be they who they may, they were confessedly, with all their lustre, miserable sinners, and one, possibly the greatest, of their sins, was their infidelity to truth in this respect. "God is no respecter of persons," and He teaches us that no man can make wrong right. It is wrong, cruelly wrong, for any man to get into a system by making promises, as a condition antecedent to his admission, and then when he secures his position and a consequent hearing by virtue of that position, to turn around and repudiate his promises, pose before the world as better than his system, and as superior in his *personal* character to his official. Nothing appears to me more unlovely than such exhibitions, nothing can be more unmanly, more foreign to true courage and nobility of nature. I do not say that it is the motive, but it is the cheapest way of securing popularity and applause to go forth as the Apostle of liberality, and especially liberality in the case of possessions, which are not your own. A free handling of the Word of God, the Creed of Christendom, and the offices and order of the Church of Christ, will bring little or no renown to an Agnostic, or any man who stands simply *on his own platform and represents no more than himself,* but when a Priest in the Church of God does these things, he becomes at once the darling of the multitude, his temporary fame at least is secured.

I shall print the preface to the Ordinal and some other extracts from our Book of Common Prayer, and then some specimens from the public utterances of the Bishop of Massachusetts with which they seem to be in irreconcilable conflict.

THE FORM AND MANNER OF
MAKING, ORDAINING, AND CONSECRATING
BISHOPS, PRIESTS, AND DEACONS;

ACCORDING TO THE ORDER OF THE PROTESTANT EPISCOPAL CHURCH IN THE UNITED STATES OF AMERICA, AS ESTABLISHED BY THE BISHOPS, THE CLERGY, AND LAITY OF SAID CHURCH, IN GENERAL CONVENTION, IN THE MONTH OF SEPTEMBER, A. D. 1792.

IT is evident unto all men, diligently reading Holy Scripture and ancient Authors, that from the Apostles' time there have been these Orders of Ministers in Christ's Church.—Bishops, Priests, and Deacons. Which Offices were evermore had in such reverend Estimation, that no man might presume to execute any of them, except he were first called, tried, examined, and known to have such qualities as are requisite for the same: and also by public Prayer, with Imposition of Hands, were approved and admitted thereunto by lawful Authority. And therefore, to the intent that these Orders may be continued, and reverently used and esteemed in this Church, no man shall be accounted or taken to be a lawful Bishop, Priest, or Deacon, in this Church, or suffered to execute any of the said Functions, except he be called, tried, examined, and admitted thereunto, according to the Form hereafter following, or hath had Episcopal Consecration or Ordination.

From the Thirty-nine Articles.

ART. XXIII. *Of Ministering in the Congregation.*

IT is not lawful for any man to take upon him the office of public preaching, or ministering the Sacraments in the Congregation, before he is lawfully called, and sent to execute the same. And those we ought to judge lawfully called and sent, which be chosen and called to this work by men who have public authority given unto them in the Congregation, to call and send Ministers into the Lord's vineyard.

ART. XXXIV. *Of Consecration of Bishops and Ministers.*

THE Book of Consecration of Bishops, and Ordering of Priests and Deacons, as set forth by the General Convention of this Church in 1792, doth contain all things necessary to such Consecration and Ordering; neither hath it anything that, of itself, is superstitious and ungodly. And, therefore, whosoever are consecrated or ordered according to said Form, we decree all such to be rightly, orderly, and lawfully consecrated and ordered.

The Canons of the Protestant Episcopal Church provide, Title 1, Canon 2, § VII, that a minister of another denomination not having Episcopal ordination in order to enter the Ministry must become a Candidate for Holy Orders and be regarded as a *Layman* and be ordained.

Whereas by Title 1, Canons 11 and 12, it is provided that ministers ordained by Bishops are not to be ordained, but simply to subscribe the declaration contained in Article 7 of the Constitution in due and proper form whereupon they are at once accredited as ministers of this Church.

Title 1, Canon 14 provides as follows:

"No minister in charge of any congregation of this Church, or in case of vacancy or absence, no churchwardens, vestrymen or trustees of the congregation shall permit any person to officiate therein without sufficient evidence of his being duly licensed or ordained to minister in this Church."

The utterances of Bishop Brooks are such as follow: The public has been familiar with his position on this subject for many years. "There are those that hold that from the time of the Apostles down to our own Bishop Paddock of Massachusetts, Bishops have been consecrated by Bishops, by direct touch of the hand upon the head: that so from generation to generation the commission to administer the Christian Gospel has come down, and that now, in this land, it belongs to no one outside of that succession. You know how largely that theory prevails, and always has prevailed in our Church.

There is no line in the Prayer Book, which declares any such theory. It has heretofore been a theory held only by individuals. I tell you, my friends, I never could for a single day consent to that."

<small>From a sermon of Bishop Brooks, delivered the first Sunday after his return from the General Convention in the fall of 1886.</small>

"I do not believe that the threefold organization of the Christian Ministry, or the existence of the Episcopate is essential to the being of a Christian Church."

<small>From a speech of Bishop Brooks before the Church Congress, Philadelphia, November, 1890.</small>

"If our Church does especial work in our country, it must be by the especial and peculiar way in which she is able to bear that witness, not *by any fiction of an apostolical succession* in her ministry, which gives to them alone a right to bear such witness. There is no such peculiar privilege or commission belonging to her, or any other body." Brooks' Twenty Sermons, p. 56.

Let me say the doctrine of Apostolical succession is not a theory held by a few in this or any other age, it is the teaching of the One Holy Catholic and Apostolic Church in all ages, by all and everywhere. Bishop Brooks may be right in calling it "a fiction," but the Church of God has held it and taught it as truth notwithstanding, and will continue to do so to the end of the world. Our own Church is most emphatic in her authoritative declarations and uniform practice in affirming the same doctrine as truth. If she is not, then I would ask any one to tell us in what form of speech, and by what course of action, she could do so more clearly and decisively than she does so now.

Moreover, it may be that Bishop Brooks is right and the Catholic Church is wrong, and that apostolical succession is "a fiction," but it is passing strange that while all nature cries out as she continues her life in plant, and tree, and insect, and fish, and bird, and beast, and man, "this gift of life comes to you by succession," and the elder church affirms the same as grace is transmitted by lineal succession in the Aaronic Priesthood, it is passing strange that the Christian Church should be the one exception to the universal law, and that for fifteen hundred years she should have been in absolute ignorance of her anomalous position among the living activities of God's universe, and that then the discovery should be made in the interest of men, who would set up for themselves and manufacture a church as they organize a club, and presume to represent God in official acts. This is passing strange.

Man can imitate, he can copy, so as to deceive himself, so exquisite is his skill, but one thing he cannot do, he cannot contribute the factor of life, that comes from the hand of God alone, and ordinarily, so far as we know, by succession. The grain of wheat, the product of this year's harvest, descends to us through a succession of harvests from the great original Life-Giver. Bishop Brooks may be right with his sneers at Apostolical Succession, but if he is, then the Catholic Church is no place for him, since she holds it, and teaches it and makes it her rule of practice.

APPENDIX IX.

"CLOSED QUESTIONS," a pastoral letter addressed by the Bishop of Springfield to his Diocese on the occasion of the McQueary trial. Holy Week, 1891. Reprinted in order to show the moral obligations which bind every man, Bishop as well as Priest and Deacon, who enters the ministry of the Church. The Rev. Mr. McQueary was a Presbyter of the Diocese of Ohio, tried, convicted and deposed for heresy.

PASTORAL LETTER.

Dear Brethren of the Clergy and Laity of the Diocese of Springfield:

The Church enjoins it upon her Bishops as a duty, from time to time, to address to their flocks "Pastoral Letters upon some points of Christian doctrine, worship or manners." (Digest, Title I, Canon 16, § 9, p. 70.)

The course of events in the history of our Church during the past few months, seems to suggest the propriety of our issuing such a Pastoral Letter to you, our beloved in the Lord, in order to allay any doubts which may have arisen in your minds, or to quiet apprehensions which may naturally have been occasioned by the assaults which have recently been made upon the faith once delivered unto the saints.

Brethren, there are closed questions in the Church of God—questions which have been settled directly by divine authority, or indirectly by the same authority speaking through the One, Holy, Catholic and Apostolic Church. These questions, which are comparatively few, relate to the doctrine, polity, sacraments and worship given by the Apostles to the first believers in Christ as the legacy bequeathed by the Master to be received and held and guarded and handed on from generation to generation to the end of the world.

From the outset the matters embraced in these subjects were to those, who received them, beyond debate, because they came to them by inspiration from God. They belonged to the sphere of supernatural knowledge, about which man knows nothing and can know nothing, except in so far as God wills. St. Paul states this fact explicitly in his letter to the Church of Corinth, (1 Cor. xv. 3, 4), when he says: "For I delivered unto you first of all that which I also received, how that Christ died for our sins according to the Scriptures; and that he was buried, and that he rose again the third day according to the Scriptures." The Apostle here quotes *three* articles from the body of the creed, couched in the very phraseology which we still repeat, and gives them as a sample of "the Gospel," which, he says, "he preached unto them." Moreover, he expressly declares that he received this sacred deposit of faith, which he communicated to them. It was not his own. He had no power over it to mould it and fashion it, to abridge it or enlarge it. He gave it, as he received it, and he bids them, as they valued their salvation, to maintain it in its integrity.

From the very beginning this was the same. The first believers, who were baptized on the day of Pentecost, "continued steadfastly in the Apostles' doctrine, and fellowship, and in breaking of bread and in prayers." (Acts ii. 42.) The faith, the polity, the sacraments, the worship came from the Apostles, and they had received them, as we know, from the Lord, and were commanded by Him to communicate them and to provide for their continuance forever. (St. Matt. xxviii, 18-20.) He, the risen Lord, just about to ascend in our humanity to the throne of God, gave His solemn pledge and promise, as He invested the eleven with their official commission, that He would shelter them and their successors in office with His divine Presence throughout all time. "Lo!" says He, "I am with you alway even unto the end of the world."

Brethren, the Church is a divine institution, not a mere human association. It is constituted by God, not made by man. Its representative on earth is the family. The divine Master weaves the family idea into His teaching about the Church, as He does no other. We breathe it when we say the prayer which He taught us to repeat, "Our Father." He roots it in the sacrament which makes us His members, "Except a man be born of water and of the Spirit he cannot enter into the Kingdom of God." (St. John iii. 5.)

Man can no more alter the character and essentials of the Church of God than he can contrive substitutes for father and mother, and invent some new method of entering the world to supersede natural birth. He seeks to do this, and his efforts are on exhibition all around us. He depraves the divine organization into a voluntary association, and lowers his language about it accordingly. To him entering the Church is joining it as one does a club,

To the divine Master it is being born into it. The idea of joining the Church of God is utterly abhorrent to the mind of Christ. It is an utter impossibility. One might as well talk of joining a family as of joining the Church. The idea of the Church is a closed question. Our Lord and Saviour Jesus Christ has closed it in His holy word. All the essentials of the Church in faith, polity, sacraments and worship are closed questions for us, who are within the fold. They may be and are to those without open questions about which one may think one thing, and another maintain the opposite, and this must always be the case with them, while they refuse the divine authority of the Church, and degrade her to the level of a voluntary association, depending for her existence and continuance upon the accidents of human opinion and preference.

There is no greater mercy for which we have cause to thank our heavenly Father through Christ, beloved Brethren, than this, that it is not our sad condition to be in such an evil plight, where nothing is settled, nothing is fixed, but everything is in a state of flux, without hope of relief.

It is true that there will often be within our ranks of laity and clergy those, who are disloyal to the faith and polity of the Church. This is incident to human infirmity, and may arise from many causes, ignorance, perverted judgment, ambition, self-conceit, as well as downright wickedness. Be the cause what it may, such persons are self condemned. The Church of God is an open book which may be read of all men. Her faith, her polity, her worship, are published to the world. The fact that they are closed questions is self evident. No man in his senses can honestly think otherwise. There is not and there could not be in the very nature of the things concerned any provision made for the revision of the government, or the creed, or the sacraments of the Church of God with a view to alteration. The bare thought of such a thing is ruled out forever.

The unhappy men, who fall thus into error in denying the principles of the Church, whether they live in the fourth century with Arius, or the fifth century with Nestorius, or the seventh century with Honorius, or the nineteenth century with the false Brethren of our own day, must be for a time endured. The Church is strong and can afford to be patient. But the time comes at length when delay is no longer mercy, and judgment must be pronounced, and Arius and Nestorius and Honorius, and nameless ones must be cast out, and become the subject of the Church's prayer on her knees beneath her dying Saviour on Good Friday, when she entreats that "He would fetch them home with Turks and infidels."

See, beloved, as touching the faith, for example, with which we are now more nearly concerned, how it is made for us a closed question to all honorable men.

When we are baptized, each and everyone is severally asked, "Dost thou believe all the Articles of the Christian faith as contained in the Apostles' Creed?" and he answers, "I do." When he is confirmed, after due and careful instruction, he is asked whether he still holds and affirms this belief, and again he replies, "I do." On this condition, with others, he is admitted to the Holy Communion, and virtually renews the vow every time he presents himself at the Lord's Table. If one goes forward and receives Holy Orders, he is obliged to present testimonials which commit him to the faith of his baptism. This he must do again and again, when he is admitted a candidate for Holy Orders, when he is to be ordained a Deacon, and once more when he is to be ordained a Priest.

Prior to his ordination as a Deacon and as a Priest, he must subscribe the following declaration: "I do believe the Holy Scriptures of the Old and New Testament to be the Word of God, and to contain all things necessary to salvation; and I do solemnly engage to conform to the Doctrine and Worship of the Protestant Episcopal Church in the United States." When he is ordained Deacon, he is asked, "Do you unfeignedly believe all the Canonical Scriptures of the Old and New Testament?" And he makes answer, "I do believe them." He is asked again, "Will you apply all your diligence to frame and fashion your own lives and the lives of your families according to the doctrine of Christ, and to make both yourselves and them as much as in you lieth wholesome examples to the flock of Christ?" And he answers, "I will so do, the Lord being my helper." These questions are substantially repeated to the Deacon, when he presents himself to be ordered Priest, and in addition he is asked other questions, which close him in absolutely, if he be an honorable and true man, from contravening and forsaking the faith, while he retains his orders. Thus the Bishop inquires, "Will you then give your faithful diligence always so to minister the doctrine and sacraments, and discipline of Christ, as the Lord hath commanded, and as this Church hath received the same according to the Commandments of God, so that you may teach the people committed to your Cure and Charge with all diligence to keep and observe the same?" And the candidate responds, "I will so do by the help of the Lord." On these conditions, a man is made a Christian in Holy Baptism, and advanced step by step to the privileges of the Lord's Household, at each stage renewing his profession of acceptance of the creed of the Universal Church. On these conditions, if the layman becomes a Priest in the Church of God, he has been admitted to Holy Orders, and advanced to the high and sacred office which he holds; on these conditions only, the compliance with which he has acknowledged, with his own lips, at intervals with years between, again and again, could he have gained this awful dignity and honor. It might reasonably be anticipated that no man who was thus voluntarily bound by his own oft-repeated pledge and promise, and had in consequence of his reiterated declaration of fidelity obtained a position as a trusted minister of the Church, could trifle with, much less deny the faith, and if by chance he was so unfortunate as to cease to believe any or all of the fundamental verities of the Gospel as summed up in the creed, it might be expected that he would at once, as soon as he knew his own mind, renounce his orders, and leave the ranks of the Priesthood in which he could no longer honorably remain.

Self evident as this seems to be, it is not always the case, nay, it is frequently otherwise. All along the line of heretical perversions of the truth, from Arius down to Colenso, the inventors and advocates of error have been found, as a rule, unwilling to abandon their positions in the Church, which they obtained on the condition of holding and professing that faith which they have brought themselves in whole or in part to deny. Heresy seems to have cast a blight upon the moral nature, and to deaden and paralyse the conscience. Its victims, though shut out from such a course by their own voluntary and oft repeated pledge and promise to the contrary, seem to think that they are called to stay in a body whose faith and principles they repudiate, and reform it. They seem to fancy that to them all questions are open, as though they had not entered a system, the very essence of whose stability lies in the fact that within its bounds certain questions are finally and forever closed. When such men are called to account for their perfidy and dishonesty, they respond with the charge of persecution and bigotry, and the world echoes their cry. Often such men occupy positions which enable them for a time to defy the Church and proudly to cast contempt upon her. It was so in the fourth century when Arians occupied the chief sees of Christendom and were supported by the wealth and influence of the Empire. God is no respecter of persons, but men are, and hence the heresiarch in a lofty place, supported by the rich and powerful, sometimes escapes, while his obscure follower, with little or no adventitious help from social position and surroundings is called to account and cast out. This is not the fault of the Church, but is due to the weakness and pusillanimity of those who happen at the time to administer the affairs of the Church. In the end God takes care of His own; the gates of hell do not prevail against His Church. Donatism, though possessing at one time all North Africa, vanished away; Arianism, with which St. Jerome said "the whole world groaned," was crushed; Honorius, Patriarch of Rome, and his Monothelite associates, in the Eastern Patriarchates, were placed under the ban of Anathema. As in the past, so it will be in the future, those who despise their spiritual birthright and scorn God's promises and blessings, will always ultimately share in the ruin and obliteration of *"the lost tribes."*

Possess your souls in patience, dear Brethren, be not affrighted at the apparent boldness, nay, audacity of misguided men who deny the Lord that bought them, and repudiate the faith by the profession of which they gained the places which they occupy, and acquired the influence to do evil which they possess. God will bring all such into judgment. Be not afraid. The Church is "the pillar and ground of the truth." She upholds it by the authority of God. He hath spoken, and because He hath spoken and for no other reason, doctrine and fellowship, and sacraments and liturgy are closed questions, questions forever settled, beyond debate for us, who believe. Be not surprised at our language about closed questions as though such statements implied limitations upon human freedom. What we say is no new thing, with which you are unfamiliar. Every science has its closed questions for those who accept its teachings, while they are not closed for those who have not mastered its elements, or refuse its conclusions. Thus the cause of a solar eclipse is a closed question for Europeans and Americans, but it is not a closed question for the native tribes of darkest Africa.

Their astrologers and necromancers and medicine men still indulge in high debate as to what causes the sun at high noon to drape himself in black. So precisely for us, who believe in God and accept Christianity, there are questions forever closed. They are settled by divine authority. On that we rest the creed of the Universal Church, which is older than the Scriptures of the New Testament, on that we rest the same Scriptures as the word of God, on that we rest the polity of the Church, on that we rest her sacraments and liturgy. These are closed questions for us who believe in the One, Holy, Catholic and Apostolic Church. They are not for those without, for the unlimited right, as it is called, of private judgment, leaves everything open. Every one is free to pick and choose as he pleases in a sphere, where of necessity of himself he can know nothing, the sphere namely of the secret things, which belong and must forever belong to the Lord our God. In this regard he is like the African savage in his relation to natural science. The poor negro knows nothing about nature's phenomena, and he can in consequence adopt and proclaim whatever theory he pleases in reference to everything. He is nature's freeman. So those who are ignorant of the Church or reject her authority, may roam over the field of spiritual and ethical speculation at their pleasure, and adopt and lay aside opinions and views as they choose. They are more than nature's freemen, they are the freemen of the universe. They rise above all authority, and own allegiance to no law outside of themselves, and this condition, so deplorable, they call freedom.

Brethren, be not envious of this boasted freedom. It is in reality wretched slavery. There is no freedom away from Christ. In His school, the Church, we are under authority, and we learn obedience, a hard lesson, but most salutary, and as we advance in our spiritual training, continuing with the first believers, steadfast in "the Apostles' doctrine and fellowship, and in breaking of bread and in prayers," the conviction gains upon us more and more, as we lift our eyes to the cross, that the service of Him, Who died upon it for our salvation, is "perfect freedom."

Commending you, dear Brethren, to the grace of God, I remain, in the fellowship of the Gospel,

Your Chief Pastor and Servant for Christ's sake,

GEORGE F. SEYMOUR.

Bishop of Springfield.

SPRINGFIELD, ILL.,

MONDAY IN HOLY WEEK, 1891.

APPENDIX X.

Declaration of the Bishops on Christian Unity, 1886.

Journal of the General Convention (page 80) 1886.

Now, therefore, in pursuance of the action taken in 1853, for the healing of divisions among Christians in our own land, and in 1880 for the protection and encouragement of those who had withdrawn from the Roman Obedience, we, Bishops of the Protestant Episcopal Church in the United States of America, in Council assembled as Bishops in the Church of God, do hereby solemnly declare to all whom it may concern, and especially to our fellow-Christians of the different Communions in this land, who, in their several spheres, have contended for the religion of Christ:

1. Our earnest desire that the Saviour's prayer, "That we all may be one," may, in its deepest and truest sense, be speedily fulfilled;

2. That we believe that all who have been duly baptized with water, in the name of the Father, and of the Son, and of the Holy Ghost, are members of the Holy Catholic Church;

3. That in all things of human ordering or human choice, relating to modes of worship and discipline, or to tradi-

tional customs, this Church is ready in the spirit of love and humility to forego all preferences of her own;

4. That this Church does not seek to absorb other Communions, but rather, co-operating with them on the basis of a common Faith and Order, to discountenance schism, to heal the wounds of the Body of Christ, and to promote the charity which is the chief of the Christian graces and the visible manifestation of Christ to the world;

But furthermore, we do hereby affirm that the Christian unity now so earnestly desired by the memorialists can be restored only by the return of all Christian communions to the principles of unity exemplified by the undivided Catholic Church during the first ages of its existence; which principles we believe to be the substantial deposit of Christian Faith and Order committed by Christ and his Apostles to the Church unto the end of the world, and therefore incapable of compromise or surrender by those who have been ordained to be its stewards and trustees for the common and equal benefit of all men.

As inherent parts of this sacred deposit, and therefore as essential to the restoration of unity among the divided branches of Christendom, we account the following, to-wit:

1. The Holy Scriptures of the Old and New Testament as the revealed Word of God.

2. The Nicene Creed as the sufficient statement of the Christian Faith.

3. The two Sacraments,—Baptism and the Supper of the Lord,—ministered with unfailing use of Christ's words of institution and of the elements ordained by Him.

4. The Historic Episcopate, locally adapted in the methods of its administration to the varying needs of the nations and peoples called of God unto the unity of His Church.

Furthermore, Deeply grieved by the sad divisions which affect the Christian Church in our own land, we hereby declare our desire and readiness, so soon as there shall be any authorized response to this Declaration, to enter into brotherly conference with all or any Christian Bodies seeking the restoration of the organic unity of the Church, with a view to the earnest study of the conditions under which so priceless a blessing might happily be brought to pass.

                              A. N. LITTLEJOHN,
                              G. T. BEDELL,
                              M. A. DE WOLFE HOWE,
                              SAMUEL S. HARRIS,
                              J. N. GALLEHER.

On motion, the foregoing report was adopted, and ordered to be printed, and communicated to the House of Deputies.

APPENDIX XI.

ILLUSTRATIONS OF DR. BROOKS' COURSE IN WORD AND DEED SINCE HE BECAME A BISHOP IN THE CHURCH OF GOD.

[Extract from Church Notes, May, 1892, the Parish Paper of the Church of the Advent, Boston, Mass., pp. 67, 68.]

"We could but feel that our Easter joy was tinged with sorrow; and we must express this sorrow here. We were greatly saddened by the strange words and action of our esteemed Bishop, to whom we have endeavoured to show earnest, filial loyalty.

"We had hoped, and Dr. Brooks' earnest supporters last spring—those who knew him best—had encouraged our hope, that no more strange utterances, subversive of the Catholic faith would fall from his lips, because he would feel the restraints of his high office, and would therefore be more guarded in his statements. But never did he utter more dreadful words, or so contradict the plain teachings of the Church, than in the fourth of his noon addresses at St. Paul's Church this last Lent.

It was a severe blow to many of his clergy to hear their Bishop declare that every man born into this world was a Christian by the fact of his birth, and that therefore there was no regeneration, no new birth in baptism, notwithstanding the Saviour's own statement, 'Except a man be born of water and of the Spirit he cannot enter into the Kingdom of God'—shows that this sacrament is more than what the Bishop would have us regard it—simply the declaration of a fact already existing. Surely every earnest Churchman has a right to protest against such a denial of the Church's plainest teaching as Bishop Brooks made on this occasion.

We feel sorely grieved at heart, and must express our grief in the way of warning against such heretical teaching, even though it come from one whom we so much revere in his sacred office, and is uttered in the words of his captivating eloquence. The friends of the good Bishop apologize for his errors of statement by saying that he is no theologian and is incapable of speaking in accurate theological language. But this is scarcely a fair excuse to urge, for the study of theology is most necessary for one in such a position of guardianship of the faith, and certainly it would be wise for so prominent a teacher to state his definitions of sacraments and the like doctrines in the terms of the Prayer Book, by whose declarations he is bound.

We have another cause of deep grief in the unwise, even wrong fraternization of our Bishop with an Orthodox and a Unitarian minister on Good Friday evening in a public service commemorating the day. We use our language calmly, and call this action *wrong*, and we believe that it was *very* wrong. The Bishop violated the letter of no canon, but he did violate the spirit of the canons and the whole teaching of the Church with regard to the ministry.

—8

By joining with these ministers in public service he practically admitted that they were as truly ordained as was he himself. And by uniting thus with a Unitarian in worship he sanctioned, as being legitimate, the teaching of that heresy which denies the Divinity of Christ and the doctrine of the Trinity. We were confidently told a year ago by many, that they felt sure that Dr. Brooks would not thus violate the decency of the Church's ways when he became Bishop; but he seems not to be guided by the advice of such friends as uttered this sentiment, but recklessly does that which he wants to do despite the plain teaching of his Church as expressed in her formularies, and the order which she has thought fit to observe.

We believe that our Bishop is thoroughly conscientious in all this, and thinks himself called upon to be the leader in a great revolutionary movement which shall completely overthrow the present conservatism of the Church, and radically change her foundation principles; and therefore we feel called upon to warn those whom we may reach against the tendency so apparently at work, which we believe to be fraught with so great disaster. Our earnest prayers will be offered for him that the Holy Spirit may so possess him that his eyes may be opened to see that the Church of God is a divine institution governed by divine laws which he must not seek to change, with a divine legacy of the faith which once delivered must not be altered by mortal man. And so may the calamity of the Church's overthrow, which now portends, be averted from the Diocese of Massachusetts.

Now, in what we have said, no one can justly charge us with disloyalty. We are most loyal to our Bishop in the due administration of his office, and even now believe that he is doing what he thinks to be right. But to our minds, by these actions he is denying the faith of the Church and seeking to overturn her discipline; and loyalty does not require us to stand by him in this. Our plain duty is to warn others of the error into which he has fallen, and to beg their prayers for him that he may be brought to a full knowledge of the truth. The child ought not to approve of the wrong action of his parent; so must not the Priest say that the doctrinal error of his Bishop is truth."

[From Church Notes, Boston, July, 1892.]

"The Church Standard" (a paper published in Philadelphia) criticised an editorial in the May issue of Church Notes concerning certain utterances and actions of the Bishop of this Diocese. While we thank the editors for their courteous treatment of our article and for kindly publishing a letter from us, we must say a word or two here in defence of what we then said. We have been forced into the painful position—for it truly was very painful—of calling attention to certain errors of doctrinal statement, as we believed them to be, and a particular action which we felt sure to be wrong on the part of the Bishop. These were no private matters, for they were publicly proclaimed in the secular press (and in one Church paper) as exhibiting the liberality of the Protestant Episcopal Church. Now, was it our duty to publish these *errors* or to keep silent? 'Charity thinketh no evil'; but charity does not require or even allow us to say that a wrong thing is right, nor does it urge us to keep silence concerning that which is wrong and being known as doing harm. It is doubtless a grave responsibility for a priest to assume when he criticises his Bishop, but if that Bishop says or does aught in contradiction of the plainest declarations of the Church, silence on the part of the priest may be a graver responsibility. But we are told that there is a proper tribunal to whom such a matter should be referred. Surely if our reviewer will reflect he will see how hopeless would be such a reference. When our present diocesan was elected by a good majority of the voters of this diocese, and his testimonials were signed by a much larger majority, and that election was confirmed by the House of Bishops, it was well known what his teaching had been on doctrinal subjects, and how strange had been his affiliations. Therefore, if the Church, knowing these things, had made him a Bishop, it were useless to appeal to her to try him for the continuance of them. We do not set ourselves up as an authority or as a judge, nor do we claim great theological ability, but we simply do this—deny the correctness of any teaching which contradicts the clear statements of our Prayer Book. The Baptismal Office surely teaches that all men are 'born in sin,' and that every one who comes to Baptism is thereby regenerated; and the Catechism plainly delares that by Baptism we are made 'a member of Christ, the child of God, and an inheritor of the Kingdom of Heaven.' Then for any man to assert that every one born into this world is a Christian by right of his birth, and that Baptism is a certification of this fact already existing, is surely to contradict 'the plain teaching of the Church' on this point, and that seems to us dangerously near 'heretical teaching,' for heresy is the assertion of an opinion in opposition to the authorized doctrinal standard of the Church. Again, we have no doubt that the Prayer Book and the Canons clearly recognize but one ministry in the Church of Christ— that of Episcopal ordination; and so affiliation with a claimed ministry which has no such ordination, by uniting therewith in public worship on the ground of sharing ministerial functions, is to deny the faith of the Church as to the necessity of Episcopal ordination, and therefore is to seek 'to overturn the discipline of the Church' which requires such ordination in order to enter upon the ministerial office. This becomes even a graver matter when one of those taking part in the 'union service' is a 'Unitarian Minister.' It does seem to us that the mere sharing in a service of worship with a man, and so recognizing him as a minister of the Church of Christ, is to sanction as 'legitimate' (to be taught) 'the teaching of that heresy which denies the Divinity of Christ and the doctrine of the Trinity.' These are the things our Bishop said and did, and they pained and grieved us, but much more they wounded the Church, and we felt it to be our duty, small and weak though we be, to do our utmost for her healing. We chose the channel of our parish paper rather than our pulpit, because this seemed to us the better place for the statement of such a subject, and because the original matter had been so noised abroad through the press of which great fraternity Church Notes is seeking to be a humble member.

"What we said in alleviation of (as it seemed to us) the offence of our Diocesan was very really meant. There is a school of great weight in our Church, of which he is the greatest representative in power of influence *which is deliberately and systematically seeking to overturn the existing order of things, and to refashion the Church on a broader basis.*" (Italics ours.)

"She is too narrow for them, and for her work as it seems to them indicated, and they would draw her out of that narrowness and develop her into something higher and better."

"We do not know the other leaders, but this man has our sincerest respect and esteem. * * In some way inexplicable to us he leads off in this great radical movement, and yet feels loyal to the Church of which he is one of the chiefest officers. Professing her faith with loyalty, he yet seems to us to be seeking diligently to overthrow it, in order to gain what appears to him to be a larger and fuller faith. * We exceedingly regret our necessary opposition to him on certain doctrinal points, but we must endeavor to be as sincere as we believe him to be, and so loyalty to the Church requires us to remain firm to her doctrines, as she has delivered the same."

[Extracts from the Boston Daily Advertiser, Friday, April 15, 1892.]

"Good Friday services: Trinity Church, 10:30 A. M. and 4 P. M.; Old South Church (Third Church), 7:30 P. M. The pastor, Rev. G. A. Gordon, will be assisted by Bishop

Brooks, Revs. A. P. Peabody, S. E. Herrick and Leighton Parks."

"Those who remember—and who has forgotten?—the use that was made, by enemies of Phillips Brooks not many months ago, of the fact that on the evening of Good Friday, 1891, he took part in a certain union service held in the Old South Church, cannot fail to observe with interest the announcement of a similar service to take place in the same Church this evening, whereat "the pastor, Rev. Geo. A. Gordon, will be assisted by Rt. Rev. Phillips Brooks, Rev. Andrew P. Peabody, Rev. S. E. Herrick and Rev. Leighton Parks." Those superserviceable friends who thought they were furthering a good cause by voluble assurances that, should the rector of Trinity Church, Boston, become the Bishop of the Diocese of Massachusetts, the Bishop would never think of doing and saying such things as the rector was criticised for saying and doing, meant well, but they did not know Phillips Brooks so well as they thought they did."

[From the Boston Herald, Saturday, April 16, 1892.]

BISHOP BROOKS.

"Bishop Brooks is disposed to prove himself anew to be a bigger man than his Church by preaching outside of it, and in company not restricted by sectarian bounds. There are men whom you cannot circumscribe by fixing upon them the responsibilities of a Bishop, and if anyone thought that Phillips Brooks was not one of their number, he misjudged his character. It would prove a heavy task to discipline him for so doing, we also opine."

These extracts will suffice to reveal the temper with which the secular press of Boston treats the Church of God.

I sincerely hope that it is painful to Bishop Brooks to have his Church used as a foil to set off his greatness and goodness to better advantage.

The Boston Daily Advertiser speaks of "the *enemies* of Phillips Brooks." This view of the relation of almost all, who opposed the confirmation and consecration of Dr. Brooks as Bishop of Massachusetts *is an entire mistake.* There never has been one particle of personal hostility to him, nor is there now. We, (I speak for myself and thousands of Churchmen besides, I am sure,) are convinced that Dr. Brooks as a Presbyter, and Bishop Brooks, now that he has been consecrated, has no moral right to be in our ministry, judging from *his own acts and words.* His friends say that he is, like Dr. Hampden, late Bishop of Hereford in England, *color-blind as regards theology.* "He is by nature, with all his splendid gifts and great acquirements," say they, "incapable of understanding and appreciating theological distinctions. And hence he cannot comprehend the situation, the attitude in which he really has placed himself towards the Creed, the Ordinal, the Prayer Book and the Church, and in which all others, who are not as color-blind as himself, see that he has placed himself."

I beg leave to remark that I would not wish to be called the enemy of my best friend, because I opposed his being given charge of a train of cars as an engineer, when I knew that he was physically color-blind, could not tell green from red. Rather I claim that my opposition to his appointment would be the best proof of my sincere *friendship for him, and my regard for others.* What would be likely to happen if my friend were put in charge of a train under such circumstances? He would not be able to read the signals, and he and his living freight would be doomed to destruction, and the corporation, who knowingly employed such an incompetent official, would be justly censured and liable for damages for the loss of life and property. This theological color-blindness may excite our deep commiseration for Bishop Brooks, but it places us in the same relation relatively to the Bishops, who gave consent to the consecration of Bishop Brooks, as the public would be to a railroad corporation, who deliberately employed men whom they knew to be color-blind, to run their engines. "Theological color-blindness" may be an excuse for Bishop Brooks, but where does such a plea place the Bishops of our Church, who were well aware of this fatal defect, and yet cooly, deliberately, and after earnest entreaty not to do so, said and recorded their decision, "Let him be made a Bishop."

I am persuaded that almost all who opposed Bishop Brooks' consecration, and who now protest against his course as a Bishop, *are his truest friends,*—those who would, if they could, save him from living and possibly dying *in a thoroughly false position.*

APPENDIX XII.

LETTERS OF THE BISHOP OF ALBANY AND THE REV. F. W. PULLER ON WHAT BISHOP DOANE CALLS "THE ALLEGED INVITATION" OF THE REV. DR. BROOKS TO UNITARIAN MINISTERS, WITH REMARKS THEREON.

In a letter of Bishop Doane, published in the (London) Guardian, January 7, 1892, he speaks of *"the alleged invitation* of Unitarian Ministers to the Holy Communion in Trinity Church, Boston."

This expression, "alleged invitation," on the part of the Bishop of Albany, fills me with astonishment. It passes my comprehension how Bishop Doane, of all others, could be ignorant of a fact which was notorious at the time, (1877), and which with his other acts of anomia, Dr. Brooks says, "was not concealed."

I may also say that the expression, "alleged invitation," gives me a little comfort, since it implies or gives reason for one to infer, that if the Bishop of Albany had known that the *"alleged"* facts were true, he would not have consented to the consecration of Dr. Brooks, and now that *he must know them to be true*, he will change his course and help to vindicate our Church from the discredit which her Chief Pastors have brought upon her in this country.

I confess I feel some surprise that the Bishop of Albany should have felt so keenly sensitive to the invasion, as he conceived the recall of Father Hall to be, of *Episcopal prerogatives*, while he was callous to the awful peril to which he was exposing the Church of God, in using all his influence to press into the Episcopate, a man over whom hung huge black clouds of doubt as to his baptism, his soundness in the faith and loyalty to the principles of the Church.

It is worth while for the Bishop of Albany, and those who agree with him, to consider what the prerogatives of Bishops would be worth, when the belief in the eternity of Christ's Person becomes a matter indifferent, and when the Polity of the Church is rejected with scorn.

It is passing strange that Bishops in our Church, and they, not among the youngest and most inexperienced, should gladly consent to Dr. Brooks' consecration, whom they knew to be at least *"an alleged"* fautor of Unitarians, an avowed Pelagian, and more than an avowed, an outspoken and blatant contemner of Episcopacy, and the threefold Ministry, *as divine institutions*, that they should gladly consent to the consecration of such a man, and then resent with great indignation the withdrawal by "ultramarine" authority of a Presbyter *belonging to another Diocese than their own*, because it seemed, and for all I know or care, may have been an invasion in principle of Episcopal jurisdiction. These Bishops wax hot with wrath, they write and speak with great intensity of feeling, they invoke the interference of the Lord Bishop of Oxford, and raise their voice in warning lest a religious order, which does not number a score of men, should overthrow Episcopal authority and bring the Bishops of the Anglican Communion into contempt. And all the while they have allowed an awful slight to be put upon the belief in the eternity of their Saviour's Person, and worse than a slight to be put upon their own order. The extent to which men can deceive themselves passes belief. I care for Episcopal prerogatives, but I care for "the faith once delivered unto the Saints," and for the divine polity and order of the Church of God, infinitely more. When the Bishops of our Church stand firm in upholding the essential verities of the gospel of Jesus Christ, Episcopal prerogatives will take care of themselves. The crowd whom the Bishop of Albany would draw to the Church by his course will magnify Episcopal prerogatives and laud him to the skies *while he pleases them and does their bidding,* but let him disappoint their expectations, or cross their wishes, and they will cry, "down with Bishops," and trample his cherished Episcopal prerogatives under their feet. There is no principle involved in the support of such a constituency, it is mere caprice, fancy, taste. When any strain comes, all this goes like chaff to the winds.

[Letter of Bishop Doane to the (London) Guardian, Jan. 20, 1892.]

"SIR: The letter of the Bishop of Melanesia in regard to the recall of Father Hall, and the statement from a correspondent as to the facts of the alleged invitation of Unitarian Ministers to the Holy Communion in Trinity Church, Boston, make it unnecessary for me to say what otherwise I should have felt bound to say upon these two points, but

I must go one step further than either the Bishop has gone or your correspondent, because I am sure that a very serious principle is involved in this case, which concerns you in England as much as it does us in America.

"It is not what Dr. Huntington has cleverly called, "ultramarine" intrusion as over against the old time "ultramontane" corruptions, but it is the fact of no appeal lying from Priest to Bishop, (when such a case as this occurs) which makes the gravamen of the whole situation.

"I think that I am speaking within bounds, when I say that before the reformation no such thing was known as a religious order with irrevocable vows, in which the members of the order had no redress from the enforcement of those vows in unjust ways. The Bishop of Oxford, to whom my appeal was made (in ignorance of the statutes of the order), is absolutely powerless by those statutes to deal with this particular question, which means that in this reformed Church of England we have allowed religious orders, and lost all check upon their abuse of power in the right of appeal from individual members of those orders, in case of injustice done, provided, that is to say, that the appeal concerns something more serious than a breach of the statutes or of the rule of life.

"Having allowed all appeal to be abolished, it seems to me that we owe it both to safety and to consistency with the history of the Church in the past either to abolish religious orders, or to see to it that the Bishop of the Diocese in which they exist has the absolute and inherent right in his Episcopate, upon complaint duly made, and examination duly had, to revise, and if need be to reverse, the decision of the Superior of the Society."

WILLIAM CROSWELL DOANE,
Bishop of Albany, U. S. A.

Albany, New York, January 2d, 1892.

Letter of the Rev. F. W. Puller, in reply. (London) Guardian. January 27th, 1892.

"SIR: The Bishop of Albany speaks of "the *alleged* invitation of Unitarian Ministers to the Holy Communion in Trinity Church, Boston."

"It seems to me that the time has come when, in the interest of the whole Church the facts connected with that invitation should be plainly set forth.

"The facts then are these: At the Consecration of Trinity Church, Boston, certain Unitarian Ministers were invited by Dr. Phillips Brooks, now Bishop of Massachusetts, but at that time Rector of Trinity, to receive the Holy Communion in his Church. They accepted the invitation, and came up to the altar, and were communicated. Shortly afterwards, another Unitarian Minister, Mr. O. B. Frothingham, took occasion to criticise the action of his brethren in the pages of the *Inquirer*.

"Their willingness to communicate with the Church seemed to Mr. Frothingham to indicate a very retrograde frame of mind. He says in his article:

"What shall we think of the 'liberals' who accepted the invitation? Were *they* looking forward? Were *their* faces bathed in light?   *   Were they extending the circuit of *their* sheepfold?"

"One of the ministers who had been thus criticised, Mr. James Freeman Clarke vindicated his conduct in a letter addressed to Mr. Frothingham, which was published in the *Inquirer*, and which was reprinted in whole or in part by various Boston newspapers. The whole of Mr. Clarke's letter is given in the *Christian Register* of March 10, 1877, a copy of which is now lying before me. I will quote from it two paragraphs. Mr. Clarke says:

"'As I was one of the "liberals," who accepted *the personal invitation of Phillips Brooks* to stay to the Communion, I will venture to ask the following question: Would it, in your opinion, have been more in accordance with liberal Christianity, *when invited* to an act of Christian communion, to have refused?" The italics in this quotation are mine. Further on in his letter, Mr. Clarke writes as follows: "I do not then consider that the brethren who, with myself, gladly stood for a moment in communion with Phillips Brooks and his friends on this occasion sacrificed any principle in so doing. My face *was* toward the light, for it saw in *this act of my friend* a faint gleam of the rosy dawn of universal brotherhood which is to come. I *was* looking forward to a better day, of which this was one prophecy. The circuit of my own fold *was* enlarged in that moment, for I felt inwardly at one with all liberal Christians outside of so-called liberal Christianity. Phillips Brooks and I *were* moving in the same direction, for we were both moving toward a ground of higher union of spirit, in which all differences of the letter disappear." In this second passage I have myself italicised the words, "*this act of my friend*"; the other italics are Mr. Freeman Clarke's.

"I do not think that I shall be contradicted when I say that Mr. Freeman Clarke was one of the most distinguished Unitarian ministers in America, and that he was in every way a man of high character. When, therefore, Mr. Clarke says that he "accepted the personal invitation of [Dr.] Phillips Brooks to stay to the Communion," we may, without rashness, conclude that it is an indisputable fact that such a personal invitation was given. Whether the blessed Sacrament was delivered into the hands of Mr. Clarke and his associates by Dr. Brooks himself is a matter of no moment. Bishop Paddock or one of his chaplains may have been the actual administrant; and, if it was Bishop Paddock, he was doubtless unaware of the opinions and official position of those whom he was communicating. The personal invitation had come from the rector, Dr. Brooks, and the responsibility rests wholly with him.

I feel perfectly certain that these facts were not known to the majority of the American Episcopate, when they confirmed the election of Dr. Brooks to the see of Massachusetts. It is inconceivable that they should have knowingly admitted into the number of official guardians of the faith one who had acted as Dr. Brooks had acted on the occasion of the consecration of his church; unless, indeed, he had expressed his penitence, and had given some satisfaction to the Church for the grievous scandal which he had caused. Had the facts been known the confirmation of the election would have been rendered impossible by the loyalty of the American Bishops to our Divine Lord, Whose representatives they are. It would also have been rendered impossible by their perception of the inevitable result of their initiating such a course of action. It is obvious that if the American Episcopate were to accept the principle that priests who admit Unitarian ministers to Communion are proper persons to be made Bishops, such an acceptance would certainly in the long run result in the break up of the unity of the Anglican Communion. There are many weak points in our discipline, as in the discipline of all other branches of the Church; but hitherto our weak points have been bearable. The consecration of Bishops ready to admit Unitarian ministers to Communion would be unbearable; and I am sure that there are thousands of my brethren who would agree with me that the deliberate acceptance of the principle of such consecrations would assuredly break up the unity of our Communion.

"One cannot doubt that the great majority of earnest Church people would feel, if the matter were really brought before them, that Dr. Brooks' invitation to the Unitarian Ministers was not simply a wrong act, but that it was an act destructive of the foundations, and that for that reason it cannot be screened by the private letter which Bishop Paddock wrote to one who remonstrated with him on what had occurred. Obviously a private letter could not cover a public scandal. Moreover it is quite certain that Bishop Paddock, when he wrote that letter, was not aware that an invitation to stay and receive the Holy Communion had been given to Mr. Clarke and his brethren by Dr.

Brooks. The correspondence in the newspapers, which cleared up the facts in the case, occurred afterwards. But I go further, and say that, even if Bishop Paddock had known all the facts, and had condoned them in a public pastoral, it would have availed nothing. I do not believe that he would ever have acted in such a way, but if, *per impossibile*, he had, he would have betrayed the trust committed to him, and an act of treason committed by a Bishop could not be quoted to screen or cover a similar act committed by a Priest. If Liberius himself, Pope though he be, admits Arians to Communion, there is only one word to be said to him by orthodox Christians, and the word was said long ago by St. Hilary.

If the Bishop of Albany should read this letter he will see what very grave reasons there were for the recent action of the Society of St. John-the-Evangelist, and I think that he will admit that, under the circumstances, that action was justifiable, and that he will consequently withdraw his very drastic proposals. I shall, therefore, refrain from discussing those proposals. Such a discussion would certainly be premature, and will, I hope, be needless. I will only make one remark touching them, and that is that they seem to me to justify the writing of this letter. Our Father Superior has hitherto refrained from asking any of us to write on the subject of the recent trouble in America in your pages: but when a Bishop comes forward and appeals to the whole Anglican Communion 'to abolish religious orders' generally—including, I suppose, the various Sisterhoods, as well as our own society, and others that might be named; and when he suggests as the only alternative a course which would be fatal to their existence, and which would therefore produce in an indirect way the same result as direct abolition—it seems to me that we may be excused if we ask to be heard first in our own defense."

F. W. PULLER.

The Mission-house, Cowley St. John, Oxford, Jan. 22, 1892.

The Bishop of Albany says "that in this reformed Church of England we have allowed religious orders and lost all check upon their abuse of power," etc. Who the Bishop means by "*we*" I am unable to say, but if he has in mind Bishops, I speak for our American Church. I observe that so far as religious orders exist among us, either by natural growth or by importation, their presence among us was in opposition to the wish of nearly all of the Bishops, or at best by their sufferance grudgingly conceded at first. Long years have passed, and these orders have *compelled* friendly recognition by their good works. Notably, Bishop Horatio Potter was far in advance of his generation, and sympathised deeply with the movement from the first; but even he was held in check by some of his most prominent Presbyters and by hostile public opinion. The Bishops can scarcely with truth be said to have *allowed* the growth or presence of sisterhoods or brotherhoods; rather it would be the truth to say that they are here in spite of the Bishops.

I will place on record a few facts: As Chaplain of the House of Mercy, New York, I was necessarily associated with the Sisterhood of St. Mary, who had that institution under their charge. On one occasion, when I was accompanying the remains of one of the Sisters for interment to Catskill on the Hudson, a Presbyter whom I knew well, and who knew me, refused to speak to me, and he sent me as a reason, afterwards, through a third party, that "his declination to recognize me was on account of the company in which he found me; he did not wish to compromise himself by owning, as a speaking acquaintance even, one who *associated with Sisters.*"

Again, in one of the earlier annual reports of the House of Mercy, which I drew up as the Chaplain, probably the first, the trustees objected to my use of the title "Sisters" in describing those who were in charge, and insisted that I should substitute instead "*Christian Ladies.*" The trustees urged that the employment of the name "Sisters" would so prejudice the institution in the estimation of the public that it would seriously diminish its income.

Again, the Sisters were driven from the care of the Sheltering Arms in New York City through powerful influences, which were brought to bear upon the Bishop and others, and the purpose was avowed of carrying the war into the House of Mercy, and I have reason to be thankful that I was able to keep the hostile forces at bay and ultimately to make their prospect of success hopeless.

Again, Father Benson and others, Presbyters of the highest standing in our Mother Church of England and of irreproachable and saintly lives were not allowed to preach in our pulpits, but in some cases were reluctantly permitted to speak in Sunday School rooms, and in secular halls.

Once more, a Canon was passed by the House of Bishops with only one dissentient voice, and that was *mine*, which placed religious orders of women so absolutely under the control of Bishops that their privacy was invaded, and their most secret chambers and their most sacred hours were made subject to the inspection and control of the Rt. Rev. Fathers. It was claimed by its friends that this Canon was passed *unanimously* by the Bishops, and the prestige, which this unanimity would give it, was used to help secure its passage in the House of Deputies. I was obliged to come out under my signature in the public press and state that I voted in the negative. It was a great relief to me that the proposed Canon was afterwards lost in the House of Deputies.

In this way "*we have allowed* religious orders in this reformed Church of England" on this side of the Atlantic. Had our Bishops taken the matter in hand at the outset, and welcomed religious orders, and encouraged them and protected them, they would have had these orders under their control, and the Sisterhoods and Brotherhoods would by this time have been the Bishops' best helpers for dealing with the problems of work in our great cities, and of carrying the Gospel through our vast mission fields in the country.

Twenty-five years ago it required some courage and nerve to stand up and say, "I am the friend of Brotherhoods and Sisterhoods." I said it, and it cost me a great deal. But I have received a thousand times more than ever I gave in spiritual help and comfort from God.

APPENDIX XIII.

Partisanship.

Under grave misapprehension some of our Bishops distinctly charge that the opposition to Bishop Brooks is the expression of partisanship.

I have sufficiently met and answered this charge in the body of my letter, but as repeated strokes are necessary in order to drive the nail well home, so repeated explanations are necessary in order to clear the mind of preconceived prejudices. Especially is this the case when these prejudices are popular and echo the popular feeling.

There are things which are irreconcilable, they will not tolerate each other, they cannot dwell together. Such, for example, are the truths embodied in the Creed and their opposites, and preeminently the truth of truths, that Jesus Christ, our Saviour, as to His Person is Eternal, and its opposite that He is not.

One cannot hold this affirmation of our Lord as true, and at the same time tolerate its denial in the sphere of his belief and practice. The bare thought of such a thing is horrible. Nor, on the the other hand, can a man, who conscientiously holds that our Lord is a mere creature, unite in worship with those who acknowledge Him to be very and eternal God, it is impossible for a man of integrity and honor to do this.

This will serve as a sample. What am I saying? Am I arguing against the law of charity and good will? Nay, just the opposite, I am exercising and enforcing it. I am insisting that truth is first, and is never to be compromised, but truth is to be held, and taught and practiced in love. *Love first, last, always.*

Persecution I abominate, and the downtrodden and oppressed of any and every name would find no readier and more self-sacrificing champion than I have ever tried to be and am. Let the attempt be made to persecute Unitarians, or Agnostics, or Congregationalists, or any one, and I am ready to do my very best in voice, and with pen and money to resist such outrage and protect them.

I mean no disrespect to those, who I am convinced are wrong in their belief and practices, because I decline to unite with them in their public worship. One of the reasons why I cannot do this is *because I love them*, and I would be, so far as my influence went, injuring my fellow-men, were I by my example to tell them that what I believe to be the foundation truths of religion, were not truths, or at all events were not truths of sufficient importance that a man need stand for them, that we may treat them as matters absolutely indifferent.

Such conduct is not a manifestation of true, genuine love for one's fellow-men. It is really the opposite, it is selfishness, it is aggrandising one's self at the cost of one's fellow-men, since it is misleading them.

I know full well that it is popular to be indifferent to truth, to have a good word for every error, and to keep harping upon the one string that "we love all men, that our heart is full of love for everybody and everything". I know full well it is popular and brings men applause and more, to pose before the world as the apostles of love, while they delude themselves into the condition of becoming almost, if not quite indifferent to truth, and to tell the unthinking crowd that "their faith as they grow older grows strangely simple, simpler even than the Apostles' Creed, it is reduced to belief in Jesus only." I know all this and more, that fills one with anguish for such misguided men, since they are misguided as to the end and aim of life, fidelity to truth and duty. Such a form of godliness may bring popularity and with it gain, but it never will, it never can bring a clear conscience, and in the end a "well done, good and faithful servant," as a commendation from our Blessed Lord. One cannot believe in Jesus without believing in the Father, "Who so loved the world that He gave His only begotten Son that He might be the Saviour of the world". One cannot believe in Jesus, without believing in the Comforter, Whom Jesus has sent and keeps sending to fill us with everlasting life. One cannot believe in Jesus, without believing in the forgiveness of sins, for Jesus shed His precious blood as an atonement for sin, without believing in the resurrection of the dead, since Jesus is "the resurrection and the life"; without believing in the life everlasting, since Jesus is the channel of that life, as the Holy Ghost comes to us through Him, the precious ointment from the Head to the members. What is to be thought then of a man, who talks in this way and allows his words to be printed and circulated. His Church requires him to demand of every one, who is baptised whether he believes "*all* the articles of the Christian faith as contained in the Apostles' Creed"; his Church enjoins upon him, as he enters the chamber of the dying, to rehearse the articles, all of them, of the Apostles' Creed, and inquire of him, who lies upon the bed of death, whether he accepts them, in order that the sick person may know, "whether he believes as a Christian man should or no," but this Minister invested with Holy Orders stands up in the presence of the multitude and discounts the faith of the Church of God, nay, the Baptismal formula enjoined by his Lord and Master, "in the Name of the Father, and of the Son, and of the Holy Ghost." He stands up before the multitude and poses as better, more "liberal" is the word, than his Church, than the Blessed Lord Himself, and wins applause and tells men how he loves them.

I know all this, it is an old story and a very sad one. It has been heard for many years and from the lips of more than one, but we never hear it from a minister of Jesus Christ without a shudder. St. John was the Apostle of love, but was there ever any one, who was firmer and more outspoken in maintaining the faith than he? His steadfastness cost him the loss of all things. These men, in these latter days, who talk so much about love, and are largely indifferent to truth, often grow rich. Their loud professions of liberality as to God's truth, not theirs, and love for everybody and everything, bring them popularity, and their godliness is sometimes gain.

Of course in the minds of men, who are indifferent to truth, or to truth that is not popular, all positive affirmation of truth and insisting upon its consequences, as compelled by the laws of thought, they call "partisanship," it is not convenient, it does not please the people, and so it is to be put down, and they will try to put it down.

Now, let me ask my brethren, be they who they may, if objecting to the consecration of a man over whose baptism hang grave doubts as to whether water was used, and the form of words prescribed by our Lord, whose acts and words proclaim him to be an Arian as to belief in Jesus Christ, a Pelagian as to man's natural condition and relation to God, and a Congregationalist as to Church government, if objecting to the consecration of such a man be partisanship, then what is not partisanship? I most emphatically deny that there is any partisanship in such opposition.

I opposed Bishop Brooks' consecration because I am not sure that he is a baptized man, (and I had no means of ascertaining the facts,) because so far as I could learn from his acts repeated and never concealed, and his words printed in books and published, and to which he himself referred me as evidence of what he was in belief and practice, he is as to faith in Jesus Christ an Arian of some sort, as to man's natural condition, a Pelagian, and as to Church Polity a Congregationalist. If such opposition based upon such reasons be partisanship, then I plead guilty to the charge. I tried my best to give my vote for the Bishop of Massachusetts. All my efforts, which I made in good faith to enable me to do so, failed.

As I now understand the case, I would sooner suffer with the ancient confessors all that they endured than record my consent to the consecration of a man occupying the position of the present Bishop of Massachusetts, since if he be color-blind, as his friends allege, as to theology, it is worse than cruel to him, it is perilous to his Diocese and the Church, and it would be condemnation to my own soul to help to make him a Bishop.

A Bishop in our Church boldly throws all the responsibility of exercising his judgment in the case of a Bishop-Elect upon the Diocese, which elects and declares that he will not go behind the certificate of the electors or a majority of them, and implies that those who do not follow his example are under the influence of partisanship.

Is this Bishop aware that the relation of Bishops to the consent to consecrate is of the essence of the Episcopate, and stands upon fundamentally different ground from that of standing committees which are, I mean no disrespect to standing committees, a pure Americanism? Is this Bishop aware that he cannot abdicate his responsibility in this good-natured easy way inasmuch as the constitution of the Church Universal, not our own canons merely, holds him accountable for every consecration in his Province?

Is this Bishop aware that the call upon him to consent involves his personal responsibility to the question, and that if there be any reasonable cause for doubt it is his duty to give the Church of God the benefit of the doubt, and not his friend, and to make diligent inquiry until he is satisfied that there is no good ground for misgiving?

Is this Bishop aware that in cases where men, accused by common rumor of heresy, are chosen Bishops, it is because the men who elect them are in sympathy with them, and hence their certificate as to soundness in the faith is worthless? Is this Bishop a stranger to the history of Donatism and Arianism, and in our own time the unhappy story of Natal?

Was this Bishop unaware that the baptism of the Bishop of Massachusetts, at the best, is very questionable, and not only so, but that he seemed to have so little respect for the convictions, prejudices, possibly Bishop Brooks would say, of his fellow Churchmen, that he refused, as I am informed, to have any defects in the Unitarian rite cured by receiving hypothetical baptism?

Was this Bishop unaware that the Rt. Rev. Dr. Brooks had embodied a good deal of his teaching in published volumes of sermons and in newspapers? Had this Bishop read any of these sermons, and did he know aught of the current allegations against the candidate for his approval?

These questions are pertinent and they ought to be asked and pressed. There is the more reason for doing so now, because attention should be called to these facts in view of what awaits us in the future.

It is a little remarkable that this Bishop, who in such an amiable, easy, good-natured way seeks to shift the responsibility, which the Church of God puts upon him, to the clerical and lay members of the convention which elected, is currently reported to have sent a cablegram across the ocean, when he heard of the choice of his friend as Bishop of Massachusetts to this effect: "Thank God for the election of Dr. Brooks." It is also currently reported that this same Bishop telegraphed to his standing committee to guide them with his fatherly advice, "Confirm him," meaning Dr. Brooks. I hope that both these reports are untrue, since if they were true they savor very strongly of partisanship, and that in a direction which is very painful to contemplate. On this head I have much more that I might say as to partisanship in behalf of laxity and unbelief, but I forbear.

There should have been investigation and satisfaction given in so grave a case before matters were pushed to their consummation. Those in power refused to listen, and while doubtless technicalities were strictly observed, still it must seem to all sober-minded men hereafter in the days to come when we are gone to our dread account (and to them my appeal lies), that the arrangements for the consecration were made and announced in hot haste.

APPENDIX XIV.

THE APPARENT HASTE WITH WHICH THE ARRANGEMENTS FOR THE CONSECRATION OF THE REV. DR. BROOKS WERE MADE AND ANNOUNCED.

The following extract is from the New York Times of July 10th, 1891, and is based upon a communication sent from Boston July 9th:

"*Not Yet a Bishop.—Phillips Brooks has not been confirmed by the Bishops.* BOSTON, July 9.—Surprise has been felt by some people, particularly by the loyal adherents of the Rev. Dr. Phillips Brooks, that there has been so much delay on the part of the Bishops in recording their votes in the matter of the confirmation of his election as Bishop. Thirty-five votes are required to confirm or reject, and as soon as these are received by Bishop Williams he will notify Dr. Brooks of the result. A letter has come to this city from Bishop Williams, in which he expresses his approval of Mr. Brooks, and that the votes of Bishops Potter, Littlejohn and Doane are for him. Further than this nothing is positively known by any one save the Bishop.

While it is certain Dr. Brooks's election has not been confirmed, it is equally certain that he has not been rejected. The delay does not indicate opposition or indifference on the part of the Bishops. Some of them are stationed in Western Africa, China, Japan, and other distant countries, and many are on their visitations. As it is not obligatory on any one to vote, there is a possibility that some may decline to do so, and these would most probably be the men who could be heard from first.

There is a well-settled opinion in the minds of the best informed that the confirmation of the election of Dr. Brooks by the Bishops is but a matter of time, and that the number of votes now needed to make him a Bishop is very small indeed."—*N. Y. Times, July 10.*

Five copies of the New York Times of the above date were sent to me anonymously during the week following its publication.

I referred to this paragraph in a letter to the Bishop of Albany, not to complain of the alleged facts in any way, but for a very different purpose, and the Bishop replied, ignoring all reference to the point which I made in submitting the extract to him, and dwelt upon his explanation of the paragraph, that it was based upon the Presiding Bishop's official letter, taking order for consecration and making the appointments and assigning the duties.

Of course we accept this as the true solution of the extraordinary announcement. But it would be very difficult for any one, unless he was aided by personal knowledge of the parties concerned, to read such an explanation between the lines of the above paragraph.

I reproduce it simply for the purpose of showing the great haste with which the announcement of the consecration, and of arrangements for the same, were made.

The thirty-five consents constituting a majority of the Bishops entitled to vote, were not received earlier than July 6th by the Bishop acting as assessor to the Presiding Bishop, whose address was Portland, Maine, and he had to communicate the result to the Presiding Bishop at Middletown, Conn., and he, as required by Canon, must notify the Bishop-Elect at Boston, and then when the Bishop-Elect's consent is received by the Presiding Bishop, he is in a condition to take order for Consecration, and not till then.

All this must be done between the 6th and 9th of July. It was possible, nay by the aid of the telegraph easily accomplished, I suppose, but it shows that the utmost dispatch was used in deference to the pressure from without.

CONCLUSION.

It is well, in the end, to gather up in few words what one has said, and state his purpose in saying it.

I affirm then, from the best information that I can gain, and the testimony on which I chiefly rely is that to which the Bishop of Massachusetts himself refers me, his own acts and words, that our Bishops have admitted to the Episcopate one

1. Whose baptism is, so far as I have been able to learn, extremely doubtful as to matter and form, since the service was performed by a Unitarian Minister, and the Bishop cares so little about it, and the anxiety and distress in consequence of the uncertainty attaching to his status as an alleged Christian, that he refused to have any

defects cured, which might exist, by submitting to hypothetical baptism.

2. Whose relation to the Catholic Faith, as summed up in the Nicene Creed, is that of an Arian of some sort, who denies *the eternity* of the Personality of Jesus Christ, since only thus can one reconcile his inviting, not simply receiving but *inviting* professed teachers of Unitarianism to receive the Holy Communion. I omit, for the present, all reference to his relation to the doctrines of the *Personality and Divinity of the Holy Ghost.*

3. Whose relation to the Polity of the Church as summed up in the Ordinal is that of one who rejects it and regards it with contempt, and

4. Whose relation to man's natural condition as he is born is that of a Pelagian, since he teaches that all men are by nature members of Christ, the children of God and inheritors of the Kingdom of Heaven, that is that *all the human race* is Christian.

I have not been arguing against these positions of Bishop Brooks, in the abstract that they are wrong, but I have been saying that holding these positions, he has no moral right to be in the ministry of the Church, and that the Bishops had no moral right to admit him while holding these views to the Episcopate.

While Bishop Brooks was a Presbyter I had no direct relation to him, and could not well interfere with his teaching and practice, but when he became a *Bishop-elect*, then he was brought directly by the Canons of our Church in relation to me, and I was made responsible as an individual

Bishop for him and his teaching and conduct, and I am and must continue so responsible until I have exhausted every possible resource to protect the *Person* of our adorable Lord from awful indignity, the *Faith* of the Church from depravation, the *Polity* of the Church from destruction, and the *rudimentary principles of the Gospel* from denial and overthrow. This I have in my very humble way striven to do, and mean with God's help, so far as I can, to continue to strive to do.

It may be said, and will be said, why disturb the peace of the Church, now that all is over, by this discussion? My answer is I am not responsible for disturbing the peace of the Church, the responsibility rests upon those who, I may say, pushed the Bishop-elect into the Episcopate with haste, and upon him who is now Bishop of Massachusetts for his acts and words, as it would seem of *bravado* since he has been consecrated.

The peace of the Church! What is the peace of the Church worth in comparison with the Church Herself?

The Bishop of Massachusetts as I view the issue now with his magnificent presence, with his eloquence, with his influence, with his following of men and women, and with his resources of money marches forth and defies the Church of the Living God, the old Church with her worn-out Creed, her useless Articles, her worse than useless Ordinal as he regards them, and proposes to give us a new Church of his own invention and construction. He it is, and my Brethren of the American Episcopate who have placed the Rt. Rev. Phillips Brooks where he is, who are responsible for disturbing the peace of the Church. I must abide in my lot and do what I can with my slender resources, and leave the result with God. Every attempt will be made to evade the issue and turn away the public mind from the real facts of this case, but in the end all such efforts will fail.

My contention is that a man whose baptism at the best is very doubtful, whose relation to the incarnation of Jesus Christ is that of an Arian, whose attitude towards the formulated polity of the Church is that of one who refuses it and despises it, and whose avowed belief as to man's natural condition contradicts the teaching of the word of God, and the Book of Common Prayer, is now a Bishop of our Church by the votes of a majority of my Brethren in the Episcopate.

This is my contention, and I do not propose to be turned aside from the issue. I appeal from the action of my Brethren who have deliberately and in spite of entreaty and remonstrance made the Rt. Rev. Dr. Phillips Brooks a Bishop in the Church of God, I appeal from their action in the first instance to the Bishops of the Anglican Communion throughout the world, and ultimately my appeal must go to the judgment of the last great day, to God Himself.

NOTE.—It is important for me to observe that up to the present moment, it is not in my power to give anything like an exhaustive list of those who gave or refused their consent to the consecration of Bishop Brooks. Of six or seven affirmative votes I am quite sure. Beyond that number I could not go and say that I knew that such and such Bishops recorded their consents.

In a crisis like the present, which concerns the stability of our branch of the Church, it seems to me a cruel wrong to the Church that those in authority should feel themselves justified, in deference to what they call "custom" (*lex non scripta*), to withhold from a brother Bishop, on his application, the names of those Bishops who agreed with him in action, when such information was sought not from curiosity or for publication, but with a view to consultation as to what was best to be done under the circumstances. I was left alone, and did my best, and am, according to my light, doing my best to neutralize, as far as I can, the most dreadful calamity which can befall the Church of God in any land. In such an exigency, the words of our Lord come right home to one (St. Matt. x. 37): "He that loveth father or mother more than Me, is not worthy of Me; and he that loveth son or daughter more than Me, is not worthy of Me."

I must put behind me all human claims, all ties of friendship, of the closest relationship, even, and count them as nothing in comparison with the paramount claim of Jesus Christ, our Lord and Saviour.

The issue presented now is the great world-power, magnified and strengthened by modern thought and progress, arrayed against the Catholic Church, resting on her eternal foundations. With all its sophistries of humanitarianism, and love for Christ, and care for man's needs, Satan is behind this world-power. Christ is in His Church, and though the conflict be long drawn out, and fearful in its waste of spiritual life and ruin of souls, still the gates of hell shall not prevail against the Church. No! thank God, we are sure of her final triumph; but meanwhile in *this land—here, now,*—the issue, in its last analysis, will be Christ or antichrist, and everyone must make his choice—must take sides.

www.ingramcontent.com/pod-product-compliance
Lightning Source LLC
Chambersburg PA
CBHW030319170426
43202CB00009B/1075